# SINGLE-HANDED SAILING

## FRANK MULVILLE

Seafarer Books
London

© Text Frank Mulville
© Text 1981 Frank Mulville
© Preface 1990 Frank Mulville

First published in Great Britain by
Nautical, this edition first published
1990 by Seafarer Books, 10 Malden Road,
London N.W.5.

ISBN 085036 410 8

Illustrations by Jane Michaelis and Walter Kemsley
Jacket design by Chris Riley

Distributed in the United States by
Sheridan House Inc.

Printed and bound in Great Britain by
Biddles Ltd, Guildford and King's Lynn

# CONTENTS

|     |                                  | page |
|-----|----------------------------------|------|
| 1.  | Going to sea alone               | 9    |
| 2.  | The discipline of the oceans     | 19   |
| 3.  | Meeting dangers                  | 28   |
| 4.  | The beginning of a voyage        | 43   |
| 5.  | Basic instruments and their use  | 58   |
| 6.  | Accidents and ailments           | 76   |
| 7.  | Bad weather                      | 90   |
| 8.  | Close work and anchoring         | 101  |
| 9.  | Trades and twins                 | 118  |
| 10. | Choice of rig                    | 137  |
| 11. | Food and drink and things        | 149  |
| 12. | The ultimate disaster            | 161  |
| 13. | Trials of the man alone          | 171  |
|     | Index                            | 183  |

# PREFACE TO SECOND EDITION

"The more things change, the more they are the same", runs the French proverb. Looking through this book after the ten years since it was written, it is clear that the volume of change has been enormous. Yet, if I were to set off tomorrow on another single handed voyage I would not conduct myself differently and would not take with me any equipment that has not been on my boat for years.

There have been changes in the design of yachts — they have become lighter, livelier, faster but not noticeably safer or more sea kindly or even more comfortable. Engines are more reliable than they were, more economical and smaller for their power. Their limitations, at least for ocean sailing, are as apparent as they have ever been. They can operate only within the limits of their fuel capacity, with few exceptions they cannot be started by hand and when they break down they are even more dependent than before on specialised spare parts which cannot be improvised and are unlikely to be available in remote parts of the world.

It is in the field of electronics that the changes have been most far reaching and it is here that the single-hander must consider his real needs most carefully. When this book was written electronic navigation was not generally available to yachtsmen — ships, of course, have used Decca and various other systems for decades but in the last few years, strides in electronic techniques have put the business of determining a position at the finger tips of any yachtsman who is willing to invest a few pounds. This may be, at least in part, responsible for the big increase in the numbers of ocean sailors over the past ten years. It has been almost as significant a development as was the invention of wind vane self steering which caused an explosion of single handed sailing some thirty years ago. The modern single hander should cast a cool eye on the blandishments offered by manufacturers of this equipment.

There is nothing wrong in principle with the Satnav. It is clearly a splendid thing for the man alone to be able to pinpoint a position in fog perhaps, or approaching a dangerous lee shore at night or navigating in bad weather or in some crisis when he may not have time to calculate a position. But he should beware of relying on this magic box or of making it the mainstay of his navigation. It is by no means unusual for the machines to give inaccurate positions, either through mechanical or human error. The Satnav can be hundreds of miles out, less of a danger to the single hander because he will know at once that he is being given false information but, more dangerously, a few miles one way or the other from the real position. This latter aberration may cause him to miss his landfall or to run foul of it. Satnavs are subject to the same flaws as any electronic equipment on board a small yacht — they get wet, or at best damp. On a long voyage it is only a matter of time before the ceaseless penetration of salt-laden moisture will cause a breakdown to the equipment itself or to the power supply.

Clearly, if the Satnav is to be used it should be in conjunction with and not instead of conventional navigation. The routine of finding the ship's daily position is an important part of the single hander's life. If he neglects the routine he will soon lose the facility to plot a quick DR position and to work his sights accurately and without fuss. A navigator in the ocean develops a kind of feel for his position which never leaves him for the duration of a passage. He is constantly aware of the yacht's performance and is always relating her speed and course to his daily or twice daily computation of his DR position, which he confirms with his sextant. The Satnav, by making navigation into nothing more than a mechanical sleight of hand, destroys this feeling. Single handed navigators are no less lazy than any of us and if they believe they have been relieved of the chore, they will take advantage of it.

The real danger of the Satnav is that when it does break down, which in the nature of things it is likely to do, it will leave the single hander without an established routine to help him find his position. Because he has been relying on it he will not have a carefully worked DR written in the log a few hours back, he will forget the formulae, forget whether the latitude is added to or subtracted from the declination, forget where to find the information he needs in the tables. When he suddenly finds he has to work a sight it will take him longer to work it. With no running record of information — speed, course, drift, tidal set, it may not be easy to arrive at a quick DR position when it is wanted. Worse, of course, he may have altogether forgotten how to navigate or, incredibly but not uncommonly, he may not know how to work a sight, or use a sextant, or even have a sextant on board.

It is surprising how many yachts are to be found in the ocean with faulty Satnavs and no means of working a sight. They rely for their position on a system I have named 'chat-nav' — ash a ship or another yacht if you can find one. On a recent voyage my wife and I were overtaken by a large American yacht who asked us for a position check because he suspected his Satnav of error, I gave him our position and explained that we had no Satnav aboard. "Ah", he said, "a real position — thank you very much".

Used in conjunction with conventional navigation the Satnav is an excellent aid but it should be used with discretion, not relied on. Then, when approaching some unfamiliar haven on a black, wild night it will come into its own by providing a welcome check, which could not otherwise be obtained.

The other significant aid that has appeared on the yachting scene in the last ten years is Radar. If the single hander's yacht is big enough, his electronics reliable enough and the inside of his boat dry enough, this may be a useful adjunct to his equipment. The yardstick he should apply to determine the worth of any instrument is whether it will tell him something he could not otherwise find out for himself. The instruments listed at the beginning of Chapter V are still all that are necessary to take a man safely across any of the world's seas but both Satnav and radar measure up to the yardstick. Radar enables him to see in the dark, not only other vessels in his vicinity but the configuration of the coastline. Satnav enables him to fix a position without sight of any heavenly body or the shore. Radar is still expensive and the scanner is not always easy to accommodate, particularly on a single masted yacht.

It is sad to be forced to admit it, but the danger of being robbed has increased over the last ten years and the single hander is particularly vulnerable to this evil. When he goes ashore in some remote and idyllic anchorage he has no choice but to leave his boat unattended. The most effective counter to this danger is to have a boat that does not appear to be worth robbing. An outboard motor is an immediate and compelling temptation. It is ready currency and it suggests to a would be pilferer that there may be other valuables inside which merit his attention. A boat that bristles with electronics, is immaculate in white paint and shining brightwork, has an expensive outboard motor at the stern and a pair of binoculars lying about the cockpit is likely to be robbed. An old cruiser, modestly down at heel is less so. Like his Patron, Joshua Slocum, a man alone must use a little subtlety and ingenuity to keep his boat safe. He might put tin-tacks on the deck, or, more realistically, he might try leaving his boat open, with a light on and a radio playing when he goes ashore. I have found this to be the best insurance. In an anchorage in the West Indies recently almost every boat was robbed, some broken into doing great damage, except my boat, wide open, lit up with a tape recorder blaring classical music.

Increasingly, it is beginning to look as if the patterns of weather as enshrined in the Admiralty pilot books are no longer a reliable guide and the single hander should consider this carefully before he plans a foreign cruise. On a recent voyage I found exceptional weather in almost every country visited, from Spain, the Canary Islands and Africa through Argentina, Brazil, the West Indies and finally the north Atlantic. The Portuguese trades, a northerly summer wind I have always taken advantage of in the past, never blew. Instead the wind was from the south and south-west for long periods at force 7, in an area which is listed in the pilot as having a 1/2 to 1% frequency of gales. In Argentina there were unprecedented floods and in the West Indies the "winter winds" blew harder and for longer and from a more northerly direction than could ever be remembered.

On the return crossing of the north Atlantic from Bermuda to the Azores and then to the south of Ireland the westerlies, which have always been a settled feature of this ocean, were never felt. Instead, we experienced light southerly and south easterly winds and fine clear weather, contrary to what is recorded in my own log books of half-a-dozen such crossings. We may be in a fluid situation where the old order is changing and new weather patterns have not yet established themselves. If this is so, the single hander would be well advised to make enquiries from weather stations local to his proposed voyage for information spanning the last two or three years and use this in the planning of his cruise.

In spite of the changes that are occuring in the world from year to year, even from month to month, both political and ecological, single handed sailing is still a fascinating exercise. In a changing world the single handed sailor may have new problems to face and new difficulties to overcome but the ocean itself is much as it was when Captain Slocum set sail on the first known single handed circumnavigation in 1895. Perhaps it will remain so for at least a few years to come.

# FOREWORD

Single-handed sailing is often regarded with some awe. Whether this is justified the reader of this book can judge for himself. Any experienced yachtsman who wishes to sail alone can do so with some adjustments to his boat and to his own habits and ways of thought. The step from sailing with a crew to sailing alone is not easy and many will hesitate before embarking on a single-handed adventure. There is, perhaps, something unusual, even odd in a man's desire to cut himself off from the world in so dramatic a fashion as to go to sea by himself. "No·man will be a sailor who has contrivance enough to get himself into jail", Dr. Johnson said, "for being in a ship is being in a jail with the chance of getting drowned." Certainly there is the chance of drowning, made greater perhaps, by being alone, but probably only marginally so. As for being in solitary confinement, a man in jail is there against his will but the lone sailor is a volunteer. Dr. Johnson can never have experienced the heady sense of freedom engendered by solitude on the ocean.

The purpose of this book is to bring some of the hazards and difficulties of lone sailing into the open and to suggest means of overcoming them. The rewards of single-handed sailing are less easily tabulated. They are essentially a personal, introspective affair and cannot be itemized. Each lone sailor will gain from the ocean according to his capacity to examine and learn from his own thoughts and feelings. Each will learn the limits of his own mental and physical resources.

The book does not set out to teach sailing or seamanship, but assumes a level of competence in a man who is considering setting off by himself. Neither does it concern itself with long distance single-handed racing. Rather it is a guide to the ordinary amateur sailor who wants to cut himself free of dependence on others and cruise the seas alone.

Most of the material is based on the author's own experience in sailing his ten-ton gaff cutter in the Atlantic Ocean, the North Sea and along the European seaboard.

Sailing alone in some respects is a form of therapy for sufferers from the disease of modern living. It is not escapism – the lone sailor must place heavy reliance on the shore both for his physical and mental support. Neither is it a challenge or a defiance or a trip for the ego. At its most rewarding it is the simple, ordinary sailor's way of achieving perfection. It is certainly a test – of stamina, of mental resilience, of ingenuity and of adaptability. To be done properly it demands dedication on the part of the lone sailor, which he will have in common with all seekers after perfection.

It is not necessary to set off across an ocean to sail single-handed – a voyage from one harbour to another is a sensible and realistic beginning. Surprisingly few yacht owners have ever sailed their boats alone, regarding it as essential to have another hand beside them, yet there is much to be learned from it – about the boat and how she can best be ordered and about himself and how he can adapt and respond to the rapid and sometimes unpredictable demands of a sailing boat in a breeze of wind. Any yachtsman will be more competent and confident for the experience of having sailed alone, whether he normally takes a crew with him or not and any boat will be handier and smoother-running for having been rigged for a single-hander. A voyage alone, even from one estuary to the next, is an achievement complete in itself which a man will be happy to tuck away in the locker of his experience.

# 1 GOING TO SEA ALONE

Man is a gregarious animal, unused to and unfitted for living alone. He depends absolutely on his fellows and cannot survive without their help. For his everyday life he needs things which he cannot provide for himself – food, clothes, his tools, his house or his boat must in some measure come through the efforts of others. He needs his fellow creatures for the sake of his mental wellbeing – he needs company, love, companionship, sympathy. In normal life he is seldom alone, at least during the day, for longer than a few hours and the majority of men never spend even as much as one complete day wholly by themselves. Ordinary life, in towns or in the countryside is a social affair which demands constant contact and communication between people. In fact to be deprived of company in solitary confinement – for instance, in prison – is a most dreaded punishment. In spite of this, or perhaps because of it most people want and need occasional solitude for short periods. A man will walk by himself in the country for half a day or a day, another will sit alone for hours at the end of a fishing rod, a worker may be alone and happy all day in the fields or at a bench or a desk. But when the bell rings and the stint ends, all of them, with very few exceptions, join in some conviviality or take part in some activity which includes other people. The lone sailor is an unique exception – he deliberately goes away for weeks and months with no other soul but his own for company.

## Creative experience

With a sailing boat a man or a woman can move himself or herself to any part of the world which is connected with the sea and is navigable. He can do this unaided, using his own strength and his own intelligence. He wastes no resources, causes no pollution, demands no services – he borrows the wind, uses it for his purpose and returns it intact. He is as free a man as it is possible to be in a world where each person depends to a greater or lesser extent upon the assistance of his fellows. The lone sailor goes free, however far away his destination. When at last he casts his anchor in some remote lagoon or ties his ship to some distant quay he can stand on deck, upright and proud in the sure knowledge that he has done it all himself. He has created an experience just as surely as a painter creates a work of art. He has communed with the ocean, learnt to live under its august discipline, mastered the laws of its terrible and awesome justice. He will never again be the same man after his first lone voyage – for as long as he lives he will possess the ocean and no person or circumstance will ever be able to take it from him. To go away alone is a grave undertaking – a man should be certain beyond any doubt before he sets sail by himself that he is embarked on the right course for himself and that it is his inalienable determination to go it alone. If he has a single doubt let him turn back before he starts. There is no room for false pride on the ocean.

## The shock of solitude

The deck of a yacht is a small place when the land has first dropped behind the horizon astern, when the light of the first day at sea has faded quite away and when the ocean is a vast and empty bowl containing only the mystery of the unexpected. It is then that the real awareness of solitude comes to the lone sailor, perhaps with a feeling of surprise. Man is a talkative beast. He starts when he first wakes in the morning and keeps it up, with occasional rests and brief pauses to listen, until he collapses asleep, exhausted by his own verbosity. For the lone sailor, suddenly and conclusively it all stops – there is no one to listen, no one to reflect his feelings or to bolster his courage. He shouts into the night and the black walls of emptiness strip the sound to a faint whisper, thin and insubstantial. He is at the beginning of his first lesson, the trimming to size of himself, the awareness of his own true stature against the grandeur of creation.

## Relationship with the boat and the ocean

He may become accustomed to solitude quickly or he may be upset by it – frightened, unsure, unable to compose himself and find a place for himself within the pattern of the sea and the sky and his boat, which together make his new world. One might think that so sudden a change from the world of people would have a profound psychological effect. At first it seems to have none but the change makes itself felt slowly and is permanent. At first he will be silent, perhaps for a day or two days, but soon he will begin to hold conversations with himself, with his boat, with birds and creatures such as dolphins and flying fish and with the sea itself. He will talk to himself quite naturally, calling himself an idiot or a clever fellow according to circumstances. Familiar things will take on distinct personalities in those first few days which will stick with for them for ever afterwards. The kettle is an idiot, a fool whistling a zany tune, a particular chart pencil is an escapologist, finding unthought of routes to the bilges, the steering vane, that wise counsellor, is a philosopher. The boat herself will soon take on a real and tangible character. On a passage across the ocean the lone sailor will learn to understand her as never before. He will become aware of her limitations, know precisely how far she can be pushed, what can be expected of her and what can be asked of her. He will know her virtues and he will be aware of her vices. He will develop an extra sense which will warn him of her foibles, he will anticipate her needs and he will bear with her misdeeds. He will learn to respect her and when the passage ends and a safe harbour lies under her lee, he will love her.

Solitude heightens awareness – perhaps because a man alone, having no other person with whom to share an experience or an impression or an emotion, takes the full impact of it himself. The extrovert sea is full of huge displays of power. It conscripts armies of grey soldiers which march across the face of the ocean in destructive hordes, shaking their white plumes and advancing with majestic and overwhelming power, roaring and hissing and spitting destruction. There is a certain sound, a kind of low malevolent rumble, full of vicious threat, which goes with a gale in the deep ocean. It is an unnerving sound when it is first heard. When the fetch to land is a thousand miles on every side the size and power of the waves reach a proportion which is quite outside the comprehension of an inshore or coastal sailor. Then again a man will experience the real meaning of solitude, then his confidence in himself and his inner strength are put to the test.

## The power of the sea

The gale will use every trick it knows to subvert and to sow despondency. A small yacht, when she falls into her metre, will ride the seas in remarkable safety, feinting and dodging and swerving so that the lone sailor marvels at her dexterity. If she is sea kindly and well found and strongly rigged and properly handled she will give off such a feeling of confidence and security as to thrill her pilot. He will gaze across the wild seascape and laugh with pride at her cleverness. Only a rogue sea, moving across the general pattern, may rear up suddenly and unexpectedly, and cause her to shudder under a huge impact of water. Strangely, it is the unpredicted wave which is dangerous. A yacht will find her way through mountainous seas for hour after hour and then, suddenly, a wave will spring up from nowhere and swamp her. Then the water will cascade down from above with terrifying force, flooding the decks to the coamings, filling the cockpit and perhaps penetrating below. These seas have the power to break strong gear. Deck stanchions can be bent over like child's plasticine, skylights and hatches can be stove in, a dinghy lashed to the deck can be broken or even carried overboard. Sometimes the yacht can be hit by a sea with such force that she shakes in every fibre, as if she had been picked up by some giant hand and hurled against rock.

## Self-reliance

For as long as the lone sailor keeps his nerve and his judgement all may be well, but a false or foolish act may allow the gale to open a crack in his defences. It will exploit its advantage, worrying and working at some weakness in man or boat until it can force an opening and flood in. Thunder roars overhead, splitting the heavens apart with staccato barks and cracks, rumbling and growling above the yacht as if she were to be taken in whole and crushed by gargantuan jaws. Lightning terrifies the night with its electric energy, striking in jagged shafts at the sea so that the frail mast and gear stand momentarily in stark relief against the wilderness of breaking water and racing cloud, lit by the eerie flicker of the storm. Then the heavens will open and the rain will tumble solid out of the sky beating against the cabin top with a hollow, unvaried tone, driven blindingly into the lone sailor's face so that he cannot see or think or feel anything but discomfort and his own solitude. In all this terror there is no person to sooth or give encouragement, no advice or sympathy, no word of affection. He must rely only on his own resources.

## The joy of the trade wind

Storms pass and the sea shows another of its varied faces. The dawn brings clear skies and strong fair winds. The storm leaves no mark of its passage – there is no sign in the sea or the sky that it has ever been, no sign in a well found yacht save the appearance of scrubbed cleanliness on deck – every speck of dirt removed, ropes, covers, white like dhobi and bleached with salt. It moves into the limbo of memory to be slotted away in the mental library which is experience, to be brought out, turned over, considered in retrospect and put away again until it is needed to counter another and greater challenge. The boat is trimmed on her course, she becomes a gay, light creature dancing towards her destination with exhilaration, the log spinning, the sails firm with wind, the gear straining easily with a vigorous, onward movement, the sea thrust from her bows and knitted astern in the even symmetry of her wake. The sun shines, the sky is blue, the lone sailor is now master, ebullient, smiling to himself. He stands in the cockpit and watches the sun fall down, watches the fluffy trade wind clouds form themselves round the edges of the world in shapes of inspired fantasy, watches the change from white to pink to vivid red to purple, watches them merge into night. He counts a million stars, bows to the moon, sways to the easy roll of his own ship, fascinated for hours by her steady purpose, her timeless gait across the ocean, the tiny bright particles of phosphorus shining all round her like a bright neon garment. The beauty and wonder of it all soaks into him and now he is glad that he is alone because he knows that a moment of such magic beauty is more personal, more powerful, more precious because there is no other person. To share it, however delightful, would make it a lesser experience.

Sometimes the wind blows true and steady for week after week – for long enough to take the yacht across the ocean with effortless speed so that the lone sailor must find a thousand uses for his time. The trade may ease in the middle of the day or freshen at nightfall so that he looks anxiously to his gear but always it blows on, following its endless route round the earth's belly. The wind-arrows on the weather chart all point favourably, the theoretical incidence of calms is nil or almost nil, the trade wind is so dependable, so permanent, so incorruptible that he comes to accept it as part of the right and proper order of life. He works his ETA a thousand miles in advance, ticks off the days and hours as the dots marking his daily positions advance across the ocean chart and settles his mind on the prospect of a fair, fast passage. But it is a rash man who counts on his arrival before a passage is fairly begun. The lone sailor comes on deck one bright morning to find the trade wind gone.

### Trial by calm

At first the significance of the calm makes no deep impression. The twin staysails hang in shapeless folds, their rounded, thrusting form which he has become used to is suddenly crumpled so that the cloths slat and chafe against each other as the yacht rolls. At first there may be a certain novelty in the silky, varnished surface of the sea. Heaving to the swell, the yacht creates strange refracted patterns of light and shade in the morning sunshine. She no longer steers but points listlessly in any random direction. The log which in normal times streams out astern to mark up the miles watch by watch is still, its clock gazing into the sky, its line hanging limp down into the ocean. Only the yacht's own motion is undiminished – free of the restraining pressure of wind it is now violent, the easy rhythmic onward roll replaced by an insane and useless jerk. Then the lone sailor gazes round the horizon and up into the sky. The configurations of cloud are gone, the ever changing light and shade of the trade wind is gone, the gay, bright patterns of the sky and the sea are replaced by a uniform, featureless glare.

A calm renders the lone sailor impotent – it leaves him with no weapon, strips him of the power to act. He can fight the storm, use his knowledge and his intelligence on a dangerous lee shore, scheme and struggle against a foul tide and a head wind round some distant headland, but against a calm in the ocean he is helpless. His engine may move him a few miles and may quell his temper but it is irrelevant against the enormity of the ocean – it can make no impact on his predicament. Now the delicate balance of his mind will soon be at risk because his mental well-being depends on the forward movement of his project. His happiness, even his sanity, is directly related to the yacht's forward progress. His solitude is only made supportable by the prospect of a safe arrival – a calm throws the whole undertaking into doubt.

At first he laughs it off, confident that in a few hours the wind will return. He takes in the sails to save them from chafe, secures every movable thing against the violent and uneven motion, busies himself with odd jobs, reads or writes or listens to music, but always with half an eye and half an ear cocked to catch the first hint of wind. The sun shines from an unsmiling sky, there is no shade, no cooling breeze. The discarded garbage of the previous day litters the sea alongside, the pencilled circles on the ocean chart which mark his daily progress have ceased to move. Now yesterday's noon position leaves no space for the marking of today's. It is as if the laws of the universe had been suspended. It is now more than at any other time that the man alone feels himself to be alone. The days extend mercilessly one into the other, the routine of the passage is destroyed, the daily work of running the ship is made superfluous. A sailing vessel in a calm, missing the dimension which she depends on for her life, is a sad, maimed creature, her gear all slack and hopeless, hanging in lazy folds, dejected and without purpose. After a week he doubts the very existence of wind, comes to believe that he will remain motionless on this same tiny patch of ocean for ever to rot and starve and die of thirst and despair.

## The danger of frustration

In a calm a man by himself can lose his reason. In a good wind he is full of occupation, full of hope and elated because he is getting the best out of his boat and himself. When the wind leaves him he feels alone and vulnerable. He begins to doubt his own ability as a navigator – he must have come too far north or too far south to miss the trade. He feels resentful because the wind has disobeyed the pilot book and the weather chart, he is anxious about his stores and his water, worried because he is behind his ETA and people at home will in turn be worried about him. The heat and the incessant rolling wear him down – he imagines that he is ill, that the boat has some fundamental defect which will soon make itself evident. The slightest thing upsets him. When he is thrown off balance by a violent and un-expected lurch and bruises his shoulder against the cabin sides he shouts curses and swears wildly – he hits the offending timber hard with his clenched fist and raises an ugly lump. He slips and hurts his knee or burns his finger on a hot pan and it sends him into a paroxysm of rage so that he runs sweat and foams with pent-up frustration. An extended calm can reduce a strong, steady man who is alone to a state of screaming madness.

If he believes that he has cut himself free of the ties and responsibilities of the shore he may find that at least psy-chologically, he is as dependent as ever on the stability of his home background. It is a myth that single-handed sailing can be an escape from life's emotional problems – the man alone needs to know and care about those he has left at home. If he is seriously delayed by calms he is likely to experience a compulsive desire to communicate with home in order to reassure them of his safety. To care for others is to understand that others care for him – a vital strut in the mental fabric of a man alone. After a long spell of calm, when even the most pessimistic estimates of his ETA will clearly not be reached, the single-hander will spend hours of his day searching the horizon for a ship. When he sees the masts and upper-works climb into view over the horizon he will attract it by any method available to him – signalling lamp, flares, VHF radio, flag signals – so as to pass a message which can be relayed to home. Such is the courtesy of the sea that any ship of whatever nationality will gladly perform this service for a yacht in the ocean.

Lloyd's of London operate a service which every single-hander should avail himself of – the yacht Reporting Service. International code signal ZD2 meaning "please report me to Lloyd's, London" should be flown from the cross-trees or the masthead if more visible, or flashed with a signalling lamp and the name of the yacht should be clearly displayed in bold letters painted on a wooden board. The yacht's name stencilled on canvas dodgers is not good enough for this purpose. Lloyd's will register any yacht for reporting, an efficient service for which they make a moderate charge. Whoever is designated by the single-hander on the appropriate form will be informed by telephone and in writing, at least of the yacht's position and time of sighting – a message can also be relayed if conditions permit. The form can be obtained from: Lloyd's of London, Sheepen Place, Colchester, Essex CO3 3LP, England. Mr. Dennis Kelly is the co-ordinator of the Marine Intelligence Branch of the Lloyd's Intelligence Service.

After a long calm in the trade wind belt, a circumstance which seems to be more common than is admitted in the weather charts, the wind, when it returns, sometimes blows from the west instead of from the east – straight into the lone sailor's teeth. It can blow strongly from this rogue direction for as long as two days and then, when this odd disturbance in the usually settled weather pattern breaks, its ending is often accompanied by a tropical storm of great intensity. First the lone sailor has been tormented by calm, then a contrary wind has stretched his resistance to breaking point and now he must struggle against the rising gale with torrential rain and forked lightning to terrorize him, and drive out of him the last vestiges of resistance and spirit.

A man alone is thrown entirely back on his own mental resources in the very circumstances that most demand communication. There is no person to reflect his thoughts or to temper his resolve or to share his apprehensions at the very moment when the vast and overwhelming forces of nature may be working towards his destruction – when he is fighting against all the odds. Just as the beauty of the sea in its calmer moments – the soft melting of evening colour, the brilliant starlit night, the magic of dawn – will affect him more because he is alone, so the rigours of the sea's anger will be harder to bear with. The most addictive effect of solitude is that impressions both kindly and cruel sink deeper into the consciousness and understanding of a man alone. They flood the soul – none escape to be diminished by being shared.

### The drug solitude

The lone sailor chooses his lot – he makes the clear cut and objective decision to go it alone. It is not difficult to find a companion for an ocean voyage, there is no lack of candidates, as anyone who advertises the post will readily find – but the lone sailor wants none of them. He may not be aware before he starts of the joys and rewards or of the dangers and frustrations of solitude. Sometimes one experience is enough and after his first lone passage he hurriedly finds a companion, but more often the habit of solitude takes hold: the fascination of it grips him and he never afterwards wishes for any other company than his own. Solitude is a drug which excites in a man the craving for more. It is likely to have a profound effect on his feelings towards himself, towards his fellows and towards the world he lives in.

# 2 THE DISCIPLINE OF THE OCEANS

Any man, or woman, who disposes of enough capital to buy himself a boat, or who already owns a boat, who can create for himself the free time and who is able to leave his social commitments on one side for a spell, can go away by himself either across the world or from one port to another round the coasts of his native land. The latter may be an excellent forerunner to the former. There are a number of skills he must be the master of, there are a number of adjustments he must make to the routine of his life and a number of ways in which he must adapt the workings of his mind to the specialized and demanding requirements of the ocean. He must begin by squarely facing the fact that single-handed sailing is a dangerous business – many times more dangerous than sailing with a crew.

There are more activities connected with the running of a ship, however small and simple she may be, than can possibly be carried out simultaneously by a man alone. Firstly, he must be asleep for between a quarter and a third of his life and during this time his boat will be left entirely to her own devices. In the course of a passage his ship will pass through areas of danger and through areas of comparative safety, but regardless of where she may be, for at least a half of the hours in the day, no one will be looking after her. This must be recognized as dangerous against all the precepts of sensible and seamanlike conduct in any vessel.

## The necessity to change his habits

The man alone must therefore recognize that some disaster may overtake his boat while he is asleep, which could have been avoided by an alert crew. He must therefore drastically adapt his sleeping habits to minimize the risks of endangering himself and his boat. He must recognize that the day is a safer time for him than the night. In the daytime he can see danger a long way off and take the steps necessary to avoid it – a ship on collision course, a group of fishing boats, the land, some dangerous object such as a baulk of timber floating in the sea, a buoy, a whale, or a sudden threat from the weather.

In the night all these hazards are immeasurably more dangerous. They cannot be seen unless a sharp look-out is maintained and even having been observed and identified, the necessary action usually takes longer and is hampered by darkness. Although a man by himself becomes so accustomed to the dark that it hardly impairs his efficiency, the fact remains that an act of seamanship carried out at night is more difficult and takes longer. Therefore, to minimize the risk of being caught unawares at night by some unlooked for circumstance, the lone sailor should never sleep at night.

Before he even starts his voyage, he must learn to upend the ingrained habits of a lifetime. It may take as long as a week for this change of habit to become settled routine just as it takes time for a night worker ashore to adapt his metabolism to unfamiliar hours. It is preferable to make the change in sleeping habits before the voyage begins because it is the beginning part of the voyage which is often the most hazardous. At the beginning of his passage, before he reaches the open ocean, he will be close to the land, among shipping all concentrated together to enter and leave harbour and among fleets of fishing boats. This will require intense concentration. It may be necessary for the lone sailor to stay awake for long periods and when he does sleep, to do so in short snatches. This will be almost impossible if he comes to sea straight from his shore-side bed where he has been accustomed to stay for seven or eight hours every night. The prospective single-hander should not be persuaded that his path will be one of ease and restful leisure.

## Disciplined sleep

Having learnt to sleep in the daytime and stay awake at night, the lone sailor must set a strict limit on the periods of sleep he allows himself. This may be the hardest discipline he has to face. No boat should be left to fend for herself with no look-out and no one to watch the course or the trim of the ship or the weather signs for longer than an hour or an hour and a half at a time. This is approximately the time it would take the yacht to sail the distance to the visible horizon. At first it will be necessary to use an alarm clock. He will find at first that it may take him anything up to half an hour to go to sleep. Then, after another half-hour the alarm will shrill. He must get up, go to the hatch, look at the compass, check the sails for chafe or damage of any kind and look carefully round the horizon. He may then go back to his bunk, re-set the alarm and compose himself for another hour. He will find, quite quickly, that he will develop the habit of instant sleep and instant wakefulness and soon he will find himself able to dispense with the alarm. He will develop a clock of his own inside his brain which may settle for an hour and a quarter, or an hour and ten minutes but almost certainly a constant period. Every time he takes to his bunk at sea he will sleep for the set period and then wake and be immediately alert. In this way he can be sure that the boat will not stray off course for a long period and will not thereby lose ground. More important, he can be reasonably sure that he will not run into disaster while he is asleep. In the daytime he should see a ship on the horizon at least fifteen miles away. He would be unlucky indeed to be run down during the next hour and a quarter.

## Constant vigilance

Being alone at sea in a boat which is travelling at up to ten miles per hour may impose a severe mental strain. The lone sailor lives with stress and can seldom be completely relaxed. Always in the back of his mind is the feeling that his ship may be running into danger while he is not watching her. Anyone who has been trained at sea will know the true weight of this responsibility – the sense of anxiety which is experienced by the officer of the watch for the safety of his ship and those who are in her is no less real for the single-hander, who knows that at least his own life is dependent for every second of the whole day on his own vigilance.

Apart from his hours of sleep there are a hundred other tasks of ordinary living and the running of the ship which take up his attention. He must frequently watch the set and trim of the sails and constantly employ his judgement to make sure that they are working at maximum efficiency. As an inviolable routine he must inspect the deck at least three times a day, once at nightfall, once at dawn, and once at midday. He must walk slowly round his tiny domain and check every rope, every shackle, every block and every lashing to make certain that the constant movement of the yacht at sea has not brought on chafe or wear or looseness. The cloths of a sail can chafe in minutes but they are only repaired in hours. If he neglects this routine, sooner or later something will carry away, possibly at night or in bad weather when it may be difficult to repair and may bring other failures rapidly in its wake. The man in sole command of a yacht in the ocean is like a juggler on a high wire – if one ball slips the whole lot may tumble, taking him as well.

## The sixth sense

Apart from sleep, there are other tasks and occupations which demand attention. Navigation, cooking and eating, writing, reading, repairs to gear, subtle improvements in the rig devised in the light of experience. In everything he does he will pause frequently to cast an eye on the ship and her progress until it becomes a second nature – the habit of awareness ingrained so that every moment is split in two, one part for the job in hand and the other for the ship. In this way he is able in some part to make up for the obvious deficiencies of eyes and ears and senses in the running of his ship.

All this new found consciousness of his surroundings, which

in reality is simply the habit of intense and continuous concentration, may still not be enough to keep the lone sailor safe. There must still be times when his guard is down and he can be taken by surprise. It is then that the remarkably adaptable human intelligence has a last line of defence, a final warning system which can give the lone sailor a last notice of impending danger. It is an extra sense, developed slowly and painfully under the stress of solitude. It is not infallible but it should never be disregarded. It is the feeling of unease and apprehension which often comes when some danger is at hand. Hard to define and hard to explain it is none the less real, attested to by every single-hander that has ever sailed.

There is some mechanism at work within the complexity of the brain which gives warning of dangers that are neither seen nor heard. A man can be lying sound asleep in his bunk, rocked by the sensuous motion of a yacht at sea and suddenly, for no apparent reason, he will be awake and in full command of his faculties. He will go out, if he is wise, and look thoroughly at every possible source of danger. Not always but more often than not, he will see whatever it was that woke him. It might be a ship on collision course, or a black cloud full of wind advancing steadily on the yacht, or some piece of gear or a sail on the point of failure. Sometimes, however hard he looks, he can find nothing amiss and sometimes danger strikes without warning – but very often the feeling is justified.

There is no doubt about this phenomenon – it has occurred too often to too many people both ashore and afloat to be the product of imagination. It happens more frequently to single-handed sailors than to people in properly manned yachts, perhaps because the single-hander has to be more aware of the possibility of danger and has to concentrate harder and more consistently on his surroundings. Whatever the explanation in terms of metaphysics or psychology, there is no doubt of the reality of this sixth sense. The single-hander who neglects it or rejects it does so at his own peril.

## The importance of routine

The man alone will find that life on the ocean is full of a never-ending and powerful rhythm which will soon dictate to him a routine and a strict pattern. However haphazard and unpredictable his life may have been before he embarked, he will find that the sea forces him to conform to a rigid harmony.Before he starts, he may belive that once free of the shore and the stultifying tedium of office or factory, he will be rid of all constraints and able to float through the long days and nights at sea on a cloud of carefree and rapturous emancipation. He will soon find that the sea ordains otherwise. Indeed, he will find that routine becomes a major factor in his life, giving meaning and form to the endlessly repeated days and nights and the vast, unchanging countenance of the ocean. It is the rhythm of the sea that gives it reality – the unceasing movement of the ship herself, the constant and ever changing undulations of the waves, the even pulse of day to night to day, the varied tempo of wind and cloud, the uniformity of the sun and the moon and the planets.

The lone sailor will soon find himself emulating his master, the ocean, partly through compulsion and partly of his own choice. He must take his sights at the same time each day, make up his log and his journal each day, eat and sleep at regular intervals – he will soon find that he falls naturally into the self-imposed discipline of routine and that he comes to enjoy it, even to rely on it as an indispensable part of life, giving shape and reason to his days and his nights.

## Women as single-handers

As the days lengthen into weeks the lone sailor will develop those qualities of the mind that he needs to counter the pressures of life at sea – endless patience, meticulous attention to detail, the ability to withstand physical discomfort and a phlegmatic approach to danger. Women, in general, may be better equipped with these qualities than men – they are usually better able to look after themselves. They often have greater powers of endurance than men and may be steadier than men – less prone to sudden bouts of depression and lack of confidence or to surges of enthusiasm and euphoric optimism. Tenacity and perseverance are key qualities for the single-hander, both strongly female characteristics. Physical strength is not of great importance. In a well rigged yacht there should be no piece of equipment that cannot be handled easily without the need for great strength. Probably the anchor is the heaviest piece of equipment on board and this can often be made light by using the proper equipment. When things go wrong, sometimes brute strength is required but a weaker person, knowing his own limitations, will learn to foresee trouble and quell it before it happens.

## No time for fear

It can well be argued that periods of acute danger can be better withstood by a man if he is alone. The element of distraction with the fears and feelings of another person is removed and the single-hander is able to focus the whole power of his concentration. When his boat is beset by overwhelming danger, from the violence of the sea or from the shore or from the danger of collision, he will find that the direction of his mind narrows to the job in hand so that every other consideration, including the possibility of failure and disaster, is excluded. With familiarity and with the close intimacy which a man in a small boat has with the sea, the feeling almost of being an actual part of the sea, the single-hander has little time for fear. He will find that his solitary preoccupation with the immediate problem, however threatening the conditions, will insulate him and envelop him in a psychological cocoon which will exclude the thought of fear. It is only when he has leisure to stand back and contemplate the ferocity of the ocean, with another person to reflect and fuel his thoughts, that he can allow himself to be afraid.

## Variety of boats

Single-handed sailing – or rather cruising – is a comparatively inexpensive pastime. Enterprises such as long distance single-handed races and special voyages in outlandish craft, may be as costly as desired and are usually sponsored by some interested party. There is a huge variety of boats in which long voyages are possible – almost any boat which is reasonably seaworthy and more or less the right size can be adapted for single-handed ocean cruising. Once embarked, an ingenious voyager will soon adapt his boat to suit his needs without spending a great sum of money. As the boat rolls the ocean miles under her keel she will grow in stature in the eyes of her owner and will take on virtues which he never before suspected. Strangely enough, on ocean voyages all ordinary cruising boats which are approximately the same size travel at much the same speed. This seems to be true regardless of whether they are fresh from the designer's pen or veterans 20 or 30 years old. Boats are a compromise and those which lie in the middle of the range between racing machines which have no comfort and tubs which will not sail to windward, all sail at much the same speed whether they were built yesterday or at the turn of the century. The design of yacht hulls for this type of boat has advanced remarkably little over the past 40 years. They have become lighter, easier to handle and more efficient to windward but not noticeably faster in a free wind. In many cases the old will outsail the new. A man by himself who can average 100 miles per day on an ocean passage is making good time. He will find that his speed across the ocean is the same to within a day or so as all the others who started at the same time and experienced similar conditions.

## The comparison of opposites

Single-handers are as disparate and motley a collection of characters as it is possible to find, having very little in common one with another except the basic lore of the sea which they have all absorbed the hard way. They have learned it in the cruel school of the ocean itself where fools are given few chances and where arrogance and pomposity and false pride are seldom tolerated.

When safely tied to the quay in some happy and distant spot, the lone sailor is not an aloof or introspective man, absorbed in his own company and difficult to approach – rather the opposite. He is often a gregarious soul, happy to share his knowledge and his experience with others and pleased enough to find himself in convivial company once his voyage is over. Perhaps the deep experience of solitude gives him a greater sympathy and tolerance towards others. We form our judgements of life, after all, by the comparison of opposites. Without sadness we would know no joy, without squalor no beauty, without tears there would be no laughter – if there were no rogues, there would be no honest men; no sages, no fools; no brave men, no cowards. So the man who knows solitude may be he who best loves his fellows as the storm is part of the calm and the racing black clouds have in them the soft, white structures of fantasy which hem the tropic horizon. The lone sailor has the confidence and the knowledge to venture into the ocean – he knows how but he does not know why. No person can tell him and he can tell no person what force or impulse lies behind his desire to shake the Almighty by the hand. The best he can do for those who come behind is to pass his knowledge down the line.

# 3 MEETING DANGERS

Sailing alone is not an extension or a modification of sailing in a crewed yacht, but rather a separate activity having its own rules and its own practices. If it is done properly it is a joy to the lone sailor and is a deep and rewarding experience, bringing a man close to the realities of life and making him aware of his own stengths and limitations. It imposes heavy strains on a man's perseverance and his capacity for application as well as his physical strength. It imposes psychological stresses which, once overcome, leave him stronger than he was before. If it is done carelessly – without sufficient thought and without the heightened concentration which it demands – it may lead to disaster or at best frustration and a sense of defeat which may not be justified. It is not all people who are equipped with the kind of resistance which allows them to thrive on solitude. Many need constant human contact, which is natural and should not in any sense be taken as a failing. Apart from the added problems of managing a sailing boat and living quite alone for weeks on end, to withstand solitude demands a set of attitudes and an approach to life which a man may or may not possess. It is no special virtue to be a person who thrives on his own company – some derive benefit from single-handed sailing and to others it is anathema.

## Preparation

Before slipping his mooring at the start of a voyage, the lone sailor should sit quietly in his cabin and think hard for ten good minutes. Is he really in all respects ready? Are the right sails bent on and cleared away for hoisting? Is everthing on deck lashed and in its right place? Are the charts for the first part of the voyage ready to hand and in the right order? Is the self-steering engaged and ready? Is everything secure and ship-shape below? Are the navigation lights working? Is there a torch or a lantern at hand with a new battery? Has he reported his departure to the coastguard and the Customs?

It is good practice to lay off the first courses to be steered and to write them on a slate or a pad. At the beginning of any passage and especially so at the start of a real voyage, the single-hander will be in a high state of nerves. Every tiny detail he can attend to before he actually leaves sheltered waters will add to his confidence. Every possible loose end he can tie before he lets go his ropes or drops the mooring for the last time, will help him to make a smooth departure without fuss or hurry. He should rehearse over in his mind every move he intends to make so that as his plan of action unfolds the smoothness of his leaving will foreshadow the conduct of the whole voyage, making for a calm and unhurried approach to each problem as it arises. This is important because it is easy to become flustered by small forgotten details. To make a successful single-handed voyage demands unremitting concentration and this must start even before the voyage itself. When everything that can be done in advance is done and when every hazard has been coolly appraised, the lone sailor can buckle on his safety harness, slip his lines, wave to his friends and be off.

## The principal dangers

Apart from the accepted hazard of bad weather there are four main dangers which face him from the moment he sets sail – he has them in common with everyone who goes to sea but in his case they are more acute. First is the danger of falling overboard which must be his first and constant preoccupation. Second is the danger of being run down at sea, third the danger of running ashore or colliding with some floating object and fourth the

*Dangers for the lone sailor: falling overboard; run down when asleep; grounding when asleep; injury.*

danger of accidental injury. To some degree all of them can be prepared for and avoided. It would be irresponsible for a single-hander to neglect the precautions that are necessary – misadventure at sea may cost him his life, it may cause other people distress or inconvenience and it brings the whole business of single-handed sailing into disrepute. The number of accidents, although not generally publicized, is comparatively high. Few seasons pass without one or two lone sailors failing to arrive.

### The steering and sailing rules

Without exception, lone sailors contravene the International Regulations for Preventing Collisions at Sea, 1972, Rule 5 states, unequivocally, "Every vessel shall at all times maintain a proper lookout by sight and hearing as well as by all available means appropriate in the prevailing circumstances and conditions so as to make a full appraisal of the situation and of the risk of collision." Every single-handed sailor breaches this rule for at least half the time he spends at sea and probably for very much longer.

Rule 1(a) states, "These Rules shall apply to all vessels upon the high seas and in all waters connected therewith navigable by seagoing vessels." Rule 2(a) continues, with a certain grandeur of prose, "Nothing in these Rules shall exonerate any vessel, or the owner, master or crew thereof, from the consequences of any neglect to comply with these Rules or of the neglect of any precaution which may be required by the ordinary practice of seamen, or by the special circumstances of the case." The countries from which most single-handed sailors emanate, Britain, France, Germany, the USA, the Scandinavian countries, have all ratified the International Regulations. France probably gives birth to the greatest number of single-handed sailors – Frenchmen, alone in small boats, are scattered in all parts of the world. The French sponsor at least two major single-handed ocean races each of comparable importance to the OSTAR race from Plymouth to New York. Every summer there is a single-handed ocean race in progress somewhere, sponsored by yacht clubs in various countries with a wide selection of yachts manned by lone sailors spread over the oceans of the world.

A race sponsored by the French newspaper *Le Figaro* takes competitors twice across the English Channel – from North Brittany to Kinsale in Ireland, then to Les Sables d'Olonne in the Bay of Biscay and then, for good measure, to northern Spain and back to Ile de Groix on the south Brittany coast, criss-crossing the busiest shipping lanes in the world. The race authorities insist on powerful electric navigation lights; each boat is bound to carry adequate batteries and an efficient generator.

In some respects, yachts taking part in official races may be less of a danger to themselves and others than the individual single-handed cruising yacht. They must meet stringent safety standards and the sailors must have qualifying experience, all of which the ordinary single-handed cruising man need take no heed of. At least in Britain where there are no special regulations, he can be quite inexperienced and his boat below any standard of safety and can sail off any day by himself without asking anyone's permission or advice. On the other hand the single-handed cruising man may be less at risk because he is not in a hurry. He can afford to make detours to keep clear of shipping lanes, to anchor or heave-to in order to sleep, to stay in harbour rather than sail in threatening weather and to choose courses between ports which may not be the most direct but which may be safest.

The element of illegality in single-handed sailing is well known to the authorities, yet they turn a blind eye, or at least an almost blind eye. After the 1976 OSTAR race, when there were boats taking part which were generally considered to be unsuitable, pressure was exerted downwards from the British Department of Trade and Industry through the Royal Yachting Association to the Royal Western Yacht Club, official sponsors of the race, so that the rules of entry were changed to exclude some of the more extreme and unmanageable designs. The attitude of the RYA to single-handed sailing is ambivalent. While recognizing that it is dangerous and that its exponents sail in disregard of Rule 5 of the Regulations, they also believe, along with many others, that it would be a tragedy if single-handed sailing were to be prohibited. They even doubt the feasibility of a ban unless concerted international actions on the part of governments were taken. They recognize that such actions might be considered, as the number of accidents to single-handers increases with the increase in the pastime. They are concerned that those contemplating single-handed adventures should make themselves fully aware of the hazards involved and of how to overcome them. There are many experienced yachtsmen who are highly critical of single-handed sailing. The forces opposed to it are considerable. There is a strong case for making it illegal and this may be done, perhaps rightly, unless people sailing by themselves are prepared to take basic precautions and to make these precautions a part of their daily routine.

## The safety harness

The safety harness is of paramount importance and its use should be thoroughly understood by anyone who wishes to sail alone. It is a piece of equipment whose virtues are universally recognized, but whose usage is frequently neglected. It must be clear to everyone who sails that to fall overboard, even in a crewed vessel, is the ultimate folly. To pick a man out of the sea is a difficult, often dangerous and always a time wasting and traumatic operation. For a single-hander, to fall overboard is certain death unless he is attached to his ship. In spite of this simple truth the safety harness is often neglected, even by experienced sailors, on the most facile of pretexts. It is objected that the safety harness is clumsy and restricts movement, that it gets tangled with the yacht's gear and is a danger, that it is awkward and uncomfortable to wear, that it is difficult to put on and off, that it wastes time and lastly that if a man falls overboard, even with a harness, he will be unable to pull himself back on board and will drown just as surely. All these objections are spurious and must be put forward by those who have not thought it necessary, through a disregard of their own or their crew's safety, to master the correct use of the safety harness and to see to it that this is applied.

The harness in its usual form is a belt which is clipped round the chest. It has short shoulder straps to hold the belt high up on the body. It has a lanyard having two clips, one for short and one for long scope fastened to a ring in the centre of the harness at the front. The belt has a quick release buckle. It was originally developed by Peter Haward, veteran of countless thousands of miles of ocean sailing, surely the most experienced and probably the most skilful small boat sailor of modern times. He marketed the harness after he had lost a crew member over the side in the Bay of Biscay on one of his countless delivery voyages.

## Life-lines

Ideally a boat should have a wire life-line stretched on each side above the deck stanchions to give a free run from the main shrouds to the stern, to which the harness is clipped. If a man falls into the sea he will be swept aft until he is clear of the yacht and then brought up by his line. He will be towed along astern, the right way up, with both his hands free and he should be able to haul himself as far as the self-steering gear. A piece of light line, hanging free and trailing astern from the vane itself can then be used to throw the yacht off course so that she comes into the wind – when she has lost way the man should be able to climb on board.

Each boat will have its own problems in the provision of suitable life-lines, but they should be rigged in such a way that a man falling into the sea can pass freely along the yacht's side to the stern. If he is snarled up somewhere amidships, however strong he may be he may not be able to haul himself on board because of the sea's drag as he is pulled through it or because of the height of the topsides.

Alternatively, two life-lines can be fastened so that they lie from for'ard to aft along the centre line of the ship, one passing on either side of the mast. In this way, as soon as he comes on deck the lone sailor can clip his harness to one of the lines on a short scope and be free to move the whole length of the ship, but not free enough to fall overboard. However, a long scope, about

*My system of jackstays at chest height. On these are
clipped the harness line.*

eight feet, is easier to work with round the deck and is to be preferred.

It may be necessary to have two systems of life-lines, one between the stern and the shrouds and the other on the foredeck. If the foredeck set of lines cannot be arranged with a free run aft because of shrouds and gear in way of the mast, it should be used with a short scope.

The fixing of life-lines depends on the deck lay-out of each boat and on the preference of each owner. The principle should be that if a long scope is used – more convenient and easier to work with – there should be a clear run to the stern in the case of a fall. If there can be no such clear run a short scope from the centre line of the yacht should be used.

## Use of the harness

The lone sailor will soon become accustomed to working on deck with his harness provided that he makes it an inviolable rule to use the harness every time he moves out of the cockpit. He should never leave the cockpit without wearing it unless the boat is becalmed or moving so slowly that he can catch her by swimming. In a surprisingly short time the harness is taken for granted and is used automatically, like a seat belt in a car – once he is accustomed to it the harness becomes an indispensable aid to working on deck. The man alone will soon learn to lean his weight on it so that he can steady himself against the yacht's motion and have both his hands free. He will learn how to keep it from tangling with other gear, he will learn how to shorten it instantly by taking a turn round himself, he will learn what clip-on positions are most convenient and what scope he needs for every given job such as changing a headsail, reefing or setting twin staysails. He will find, once he is used to it, that he feels undressed and insecure on deck without it and therefore unable to work efficiently.

Falling overboard is an ever-present danger which can happen to anyone even in sheltered estuaries and coastal waters. The motion of a yacht in the deep ocean in a gale of wind is something quite outside the experience of normal week-end

*The man alone will soon learn to lean his weight against a harness and have both hands free.*

and holiday sailing and in those circumstances, precautions which may seem at first sight to be fussy and over cautious, become no more than common, sensible seamanship.

**Checking the design**

It is important that the harness is a good one and that the lanyard is strong enough to withstand the heavy strain of towing a man through the water at speed. The greatest care must be taken by the single-hander with the harness's lanyard – almost

37

every harness available is wrongly designed and should immediately be modified. The lanyard must be capable of being let go from the harness, when under heavy strain or the single-hander may be dragged to his death. It should not be spliced to the harness ring or fastened with an ordinary spring clip or it may be impossible to undo. Rather a quick release shackle should be used which can be let go when under strain. In no circumstances should the lanyard ever be taken off the harness or stowed separately from it. Some harness manufacturers actually recommend this, but it is folly. In an emergency the harness could be put on and the lanyard left below, rendering the harness useless. Another common fault is that the ring is too

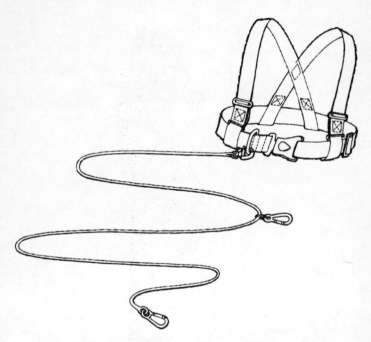

*Safety harness: the single-hander's literal line of life. Stitching should be supplemented, if necessary. A quick release shackle (not a carbine hook) should be fitted to the inner end.*

high on the harness so that when being towed along, the shoulder straps or the ring itself will press against the face painfully and force the head back. Ideally, the ring should be fastened to the belt itself which is the strongest anchorage for it. For the sake of security it is worth hand stitching over the very thin nylon stitching used in the make-up of most standard harnesses.

## Stowage for the harness

When not in use it should be kept stowed in such a way that it is always instantly available. For preference it should be stowed

*Harness ready below deck, complete with its line ready to be donned instantly.*

carefully on a hook, well clear of the other gear. The clasp should be left done up when the harness is not in use. In this way the harness will never be inside out when wanted.

Each person in a crewed yacht should have his own harness, which he should use exclusively, so that he can come to it in the dark and know that it will be just where he left it, ready for use. It should never be necessary to use a light in order to get into the harness as this impairs night eyesight – with practice the whole operation is done in one minute at the longest and this short interval of time itself is often useful. A man who gets out of his bunk at night to reef or to change a sail can get much good out of a minute in which to think about what he is going to do and how he is going to do it.

## Testing the harness

The safety harness should be tested in calm waters on a fine sunny day with a companion on board, before a single-handed voyage begins. This should be done on different points of sailing and at different speeds. The prospective single-hander should simulate a slip from various points around the yacht and see for himself how easy or difficult it is to regain the deck. Sometimes a short length of rope hanging overboard at the chain plates is a help, it may be useful to position a ladder permanently over the stern or a rope hanging in a shallow bight from the bow to amidships. Each boat varies as does the strength and athletic prowess of each person and a few well thought-out aids, positioned in advance against such an emergency, may make the difference between life and death. Some single-handers tow a length of rope permanently over the stern but this is no substitute for a harness. The pressure of water is so great at five or six knots that it is impossible for a man to haul himself against it along a rope. Only with a harness with its lanyard fastened well above the deck, has a man the slightest chance of climbing back on board a fast moving yacht.

The danger of falling overboard is no less, possibly greater in a yacht with two or more people on board. The single-hander with some experience behind him is acutely aware of the danger

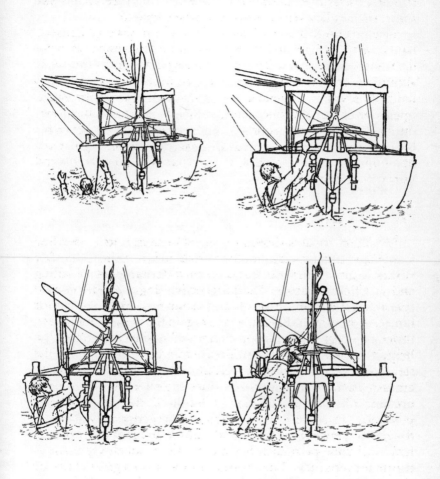

*Test your ability to regain the deck, for instance by climbing over the self-steering vane and rudder. A lanyard hanging loose from this vane will enable the yacht to be brought into the wind.*

and is on his guard. In a crewed yacht a man may be careless in
the belief that if he does fall he will soon be picked up – no
assumption could be less justified. A man who falls from a yacht
is very fortunate if he is picked up. At night, even if the watch
below wakes immediately, a man in the sea will be out of sight
within minutes, even seconds. In a strong following trade wind
with twins set and the gear made up for running it will be miles
before way can be taken off and the yacht turned to windward.
Even on a clear, calm day it is very difficult to see a man in the sea
until he is close alongside – at night or in rough weather his
chances are minimal. The man alone has no chance.

## The lesson

It may take a disaster or a near disaster to drive the lesson
home – a man who has fallen from a yacht in the ocean and has
survived will know the value of a safety harness as will a skipper,
like Peter Haward, who has lost a man at sea. Disaster usually
strikes without warning. A man alone, changing a sail on the
foredeck in bad weather whilst his boat sails herself, can become
absorbed in the job and careless of his own safety. He can reach
out to grasp an elusive rope's end or balance momentarily to
unfasten a knot which is almost too high for him. At that precise
moment a rogue swell gives the yacht a sudden and unpredicted
lurch and all at once the lone sailor finds his balance gone and
his body out of control. Then he will have a sensation of utter
loneliness as the magnitude of his folly is thrust on his consciousness – a sick feeling of cold fear flushes through his mind.
In a second the ordered routine of his life is put at risk. He flays
out with his arms wildly in a vain effort to regain balance or to
find some rope or spar or shroud to catch a hold. Then the yacht
swings suddenly the other way, the rail flips the back of his legs
and he is over backwards into the sea. He breaks surface in time
to see the shining, smooth topside flash past his eyes. He gropes
vainly upwards but the painted, uniform surface offers no
possible hold, the yacht's quarter wave washes him clear of the
stern and suddenly he is alone in the ocean, left with the
enormity of his folly as the yacht sails into infinity.

# 4 THE BEGINNING OF A VOYAGE

It was Hasler's invention, or to be more precise his adaptation, of a self-steering gear operated by the wind that made single-handed sailing popular. Hasler's brainchild came from vane steering gears he saw on model yachts on the Round Pond in Kensington Gardens.

Suddenly, after Hasler, sailing in boats that steer themselves by the wind opened huge new opportunities for the single-hander. No longer was a man tied to the helm day and night unless he chose to put his trust in some improvised arrangement for steering. Now the single-hander could leave his boat to her own devices for hours, days or weeks in the knowledge that she would stay at a constant angle to the direction of the wind. It would be an interesting exercise to reconstruct a single-handed voyage using a yacht of modern design without any form of mechanical self-steering in order to assess the impact of this most significant invention.

The single-handed circumnavigators of the past, Joshua Slocum, Harry Pidgeon, Alain Gerbault, Vito Dumas, achieved their astonishing voyages without this equipment. They made their boats steer themselves by a variety of means, with sheets led to the helm from mainsail or staysail or twins, and with compensating elastic or check lines or even counterweights. *Spray*, according to Slocum, was so perfectly balanced that she steered herself for thousands of miles with no other assistance than a line round the tiller. He recounts that she sailed for a month across the Pacific from Chile to the Marquesas without a hand touching the helm. Although it is fashionable to take this first and greatest single-hander's claims with a pinch of salt, this story may well be true. Heavy boats with long, straight keels are remarkably steady and can be made to steer themselves for long periods, provided that the wind also remains steady. But there is no measure of certainty with this method. Even with a good, vane-operated steering gear a boat can stray off course if the wind shifts or alters substantially in strength – without a gear most single-handed yachts would be all over the ocean while the skipper was asleep.

### Self-steering gears

In some respects electrically-operated gears which keep the yacht on a steady compass course are an advantage – they may be useful when sailing near the coast where the wind may be fluky and when it is important not to deviate and for steering when there is no wind. This type of equipment uses the ship's battery power and is subject to mechanical and electrical failure but it would be an advantage for a single-hander to have both. A reliable steering gear is perhaps the most important piece of equipment on board a single-handed yacht. It takes over a time-consuming and tiresome chore which is also perhaps the most important activity on board. A good steering gear is the single-hander's best friend – it does its work competently and without fuss. It doesn't eat or smoke or drink or misbehave in port.

### The log book

The first part of a voyage will be in an estuary or along the coast or in constricted waters where there will be shipping to be avoided and where intricate navigation will be needed. As soon as he clears the harbour wall, has all his harbour gear stowed and is in all respects ready for the voyage, the single-hander should open his log book and mark down, COP – commencement of passage. The log book is also a vital piece of equipment. It is essential to use it properly, recording all the information which is needed to compile the ship's DR position, all information which is of relevance to the voyage and avoiding such miscellanies as impressions or thoughts or feelings which should be reserved for another volume, of almost equal importance, the ship's journal.

There are many types of printed log book available – most of them have the defect of being too complicated, too comprehensive and, occasionally, pretentious. Conciseness and simplicity should be aimed at. An exercise book with a stiff cover is as good as anything, which can be ruled up as convenient. The double spread of the book should be used, with columns ruled for routine information on the left-hand page and "remarks" on the right. The day and the date should be written across the ruled columns and underlined so that it can easily be turned to for reference. Essential column headings are, 1. ST (ship's time); 2. Course (magnetic); 3. Barom. (barometric reading, preferably in millibars); 4. $\triangle$ (the symbol for log reading, derived from the log-ship of ancient times); 5. Wind direction and strength; 6. Engine time (this should be a cumulative total to give an accurate record of the total number of hours the engine has run since the beginning of the voyage or since refuelling). These are essentials but each person will have his preference. It is worth having a column for the distance run each day by log and the actual distance run between sights. Also, to give encouragement, it is worth recording each day the total distance run on the passage. On the opposite page under "Remarks" there should be a record of the state of the sea, the sail that is carried, when reefs are taken in and let out, when the engine is started and stopped, when ships are sighted and their names if possible. When coasting there should be a record of what lights or marks are in view and the times they are passed. The memory is fallible — the single-hander has no one to ask or consult and therefore he must have a proper record of every day and every hour that passes.

## Making up the dead reckoning

When coasting, perhaps at the beginning or towards the end

45

of a passage, the patent log should be read and a position marked on the chart every two hours. A fixed position which has been determined by bearings or by sights should be marked on the chart with a ring ⊙ and an estimated position, perhaps with a single bearing combined with a log reading and an allowance for current or tidal stream, should be marked with a cross X. It is most important when sailing near a coast that before he goes to sleep either by day or by night, the single-hander should note the time and log reading so that when he wakes he will have some idea of what his boat has been up to. The DR must always be kept up to date and marked on the chart at frequent intervals. To reconstruct a DR position after a day's run, even if all the details of alterations in course and speed have been carefully noted, is a laborious business which is open to error. A DR position which is frequently plotted is easy to maintain and is more likely to be accurate.

## Frequent log entries

It is surprising how quickly the time passes for a man alone at sea and surprising how capricious the memory can be. Details of set and current and tidal stream must be incorporated in the DR calculation frequently. Anything that will serve to give a position line should be used – a light, a sea mark, even a crossing ferry travelling to a known destination should be logged. Ships on a known sea route, for instance between Ushant and Cape Finisterre can give an excellent indication of longitude. Even an aeroplane passing overhead might serve to confirm a position line although, of course, no reliance should be placed on such nebulous hints. At any time of the day or night the single-hander might find himself dealing with several pressing problems at the same time. It helps if he is at all times sure of his position.

Before the voyage begins, the standard, or master compass must be adjusted and a deviation card made out. The single-hander should also check the hand bearing compass. This can be done most simply by taking cross bearings from the mooring, or from a fixed point on land which is marked on the chart such as the end of a harbour mole, or by comparing it with the master compass if that is known to be correct. The log should also be checked between shore bearings, making due allowance for the tide. Soon, the single-hander will develop a talent born of experience, taking into account all the facts and all the indications and adding to them the further, intangible ingredient which is an intuitive, shrewd guess. A boat sailed by a man alone is subject to variations of course and speed and drift which cannot be evaluated accurately. The single-hander will learn to apply the idiosyncracies of his boat, the weather and the conditions to his DR position with a surprising degree of accuracy. It is this facility to feel for a position almost by instinctive perception, which distinguishes the good navigator. Equally, such things as perceptions and intuitions can be and often are wrong. They should never be allowed to detract from the validity of a truly observed and properly calculated and laid off position. It is this that will appear on the chart.

## Charts

Deciding what charts to put aboard at the beginning of a voyage is always difficult – there are considerations of expense and space and facilities for keeping them up to date. There is no doubt that adequate charts are a major comfort for the single-hander. Striving to gain harbour on some unfamiliar shore he will be immensely helped by having the right large scale chart – he may curse his own parsimony if he is without. If the voyage is a carefully planned one, he will want small scale charts of all the sea areas he is likely to pass through and large scale charts of the coasts and harbours he plans to visit. On a long voyage, he may have to spend a fair sum of money on charts unless, by judicious advertising or by luck, he is able to contact another yacht making a similar voyage at a different time so that charts can be sent from the first out to the second and the expenditure halved. To save space a yacht leaving European waters bound south or west can leave a parcel of charts ashore, for instance in Vigo, Spain, which can then be collected again on the return journey. It is often possible to leave charts at an official chart depot where they are stored in safety and kept up to date for a small sum. Alternatively, it is possible to arrange for Notices to Mariners to be forwarded to a yacht at regular intervals.

## Coasting

It should not be difficult for the single hander to keep clear of shipping in coastal waters – paradoxically, the danger of collision with a ship is greater in the open ocean. Coastal shipping keeps to well defined lanes and provided the single-hander keeps clear of them he should have no problem. Entering and leaving harbours or crossing the shipping lanes he will be up and alert so that his natural commonsense and his knowledge of the rule of the road should be all that he requires. In settled weather when coasting it is often possible to move into shallower water and thus be certain of not being run down by a ship.

Fishing boats are more difficult to avoid than ships and are a greater threat to the single-hander – they travel fast when going to and from their fishing grounds and are notorious for not keeping a proper look-out. When they are actually fishing they are not bound by the regulations to keep out of a yacht's way. Fleets of fishermen are usually to be found on or around banks or shallows off the coast but sometimes they operate hundreds of miles off-shore. A look at the chart will usually show where they are most likely to be, but there are always strays far away from the main fleet or making the passage to or from their base. It is worth remembering that a fishing boat which fails to keep a proper look-out is committing no worse a crime than the single-hander himself.

Small line-fishing boats with outboard motors often venture far out to sea in settled weather and may lie at anchor or drift with the tide. They often cannot be seen until they are close aboard and are a considerable hazard to the single-hander. He must also be on the watch for buoys, which are easily run into and for oil rigs which may not be marked on the chart. The current notices to mariners carry details of the positions of oil rigs and these are worth marking on the chart so that they can be given a wide berth. Once among rigs there can be no rest for the single-hander.

## Sleep when coasting

Getting enough sleep when sailing near the coast may be the lone sailor's greatest problem. It is often possible to make harbour every night until an offing can be gained and the coastline cleared but this is time wasting and not always acceptable. If he is anxious to get on with his voyage he will stay at sea to avoid the delays and inconvenience of entering and leaving harbour and to avoid upsetting his sea routine. It is often possible to anchor on some sandbank offshore to sleep for an hour or so and, possibly, to save a foul tide at the same time. Equally, in settled weather, he can anchor near the shore provided the holding ground is good and there is no chance of a hard onshore wind.

The chances are, however, that he will at some time near the beginning of his voyage find himself among shipping or close to the shore and at the same time needing sleep. To sleep regularly and well is imperative – without it the judgement to make the right decisions is impaired as well as the physical capacity to carry those decisions out. In the daytime in fair weather, it is usually possible to find a piece of sea clear enough and far enough off-shore to allow for an hour's sleep but at night this may be difficult, particularly in unpleasant weather. It is here that the routine of sleeping in short snatches, mainly during the day, is most essential. It might be advisable to shorten sail in order to take way off the boat or even to heave-to when rest is needed. The paramount rule which must never be disregarded is never to sleep when the boat is close to the shore if there is any possibility that she could come up with the shore during the period of sleep. It is remarkable how many boats have been lost through running ashore while their crews have been asleep.

## Lights

At night, particularly near the coast, the single-hander must carry lights that can be seen by another vessel a long way off. The side-lights that are carried by many yachts, either fixed to the pulpit or on boards in the shrouds, are of doubtful usefulness. They may comply with the regulations and they may be adequate in calm weather, but they are often not powerful enough or well enough positioned to make a real mark on a stormy night. They are easily obscured by the yacht's sails and when she is heeling they shine either down into the sea or at the stars. An electric tri-colour lantern at the mast head is now legalized, but even this may be inadequate for the single-hander – theoretically it can be seen five miles off but it is a tiny pinpoint of light in the ocean, waving wildly from side to side and difficult to identify from the bridge of a ship.

A useful supplement to the regulation lights, whether masthead or side-lights, is a paraffin pressure lantern hung on the boom gallows or the backstay below the level of the boom, or in any part of the ship from where it can be seen all round the horizon. It should be positioned where it is clear of Terylene (Dacron) or nylon rope or sails which are inflammable. This will bathe the whole yacht and the surrounding sea in a pool of light which can be readily seen. It will illuminate the sails so that she can be identified as a yacht and it will make a larger, steadier pool of light which has a greater chance of being seen.

## Electric and oil lights

A powerful electric torch or better still a daylight signalling lamp powered by the ship's batteries is essential in crowded waters. In an emergency it should be pointed directly at the bridge of another vessel on collision course and held steady. Directing a torch or lamp on the sails has very little effect – it shows up well from on board the yacht, but not from any distance off, because the light is reflected as opposed to the direct beam of a signalling lamp.

It is unwise to rely only on electric power on board – failures to the whole system due to a flat battery or a single faulty connection are not uncommon and failures of individual pieces of electric equipment are frequent. On a long sea passage in a yacht

*In mid-ocean a paraffin pressure lamp hung in boom gallows is a good way to draw attention to the yacht at night. Closer to land, correct navigation lights must be shown.*

all electrical or electronic fittings must be suspect. They all suffer from corrosion to some degree either as a result of a thorough soaking in sea water or the ceaseless disintegration caused by damp, salt air. In addition, the single-hander will be parsimonious with his supplies of fuel, and will not wish to run his engine or his generator to charge batteries for longer than is necessary. Oil navigation lights should always be carried on a long passage when the engine is seldom used. The best position for them is on the coach roof immediately forward of the cockpit where they can easily be reached for lighting and frequent inspection. The two systems, oil and electric, should be used side by side. The oil lamps should be lit at sunset as a matter of course and the electrics should be held in reserve to be flashed on when extra power is needed.

The care and maintenance of oil lamps should be taken seriously by the single-hander because oil lighting is a great convenience and a comfort not to be equalled by the most expensive or sophisticated electrical systems. This is not to detract from the value of electrics – the oil system is a supplement which can save hours of generator time or main engine time. If oil lighting is used wisely it should not be necessary either to carry a separate generator or to use the main engine other than for propulsion. A good supply of paraffin (or lamp oil) should be carried in a proper storage tank, preferably of galvanized iron because in many countries the quality of the oil is poor, causing lamps to burn with a dirty, smoky flame. As well as port and starboard and stern lights and a pressure lamp, there should be at least two oil lamps inside the cabin. The oil cabin lamps are indispensable for the single-hander. They give a soft, soothing light which does not dazzle or unduly impair night eyesight and they give a welcome measure of warmth to the cabin. For reading or chartwork at night in congested waters low power electric lights can be briefly used, but an oil lamp should be left on all night. If the single-hander is called out suddenly in answer to some alarm his eyesight will then be attuned to the darkness and he will not waste valuable minutes. From ordinary electric cabin lighting it takes 20 minutes for the eyes to accustom themselves to a dark night.

Lamps are difficult to fill when the boat is moving briskly in a rough sea. The best method is to first transfer oil from the tank to a transparent plastic container of about 1 gallon capacity, which will last the ship for several days. The cabin lamps can be filled direct from the container if it has an efficient pourer, but the navigation lights are too small and fiddly. They should be filled from a small plastic bottle with a fine tube fitted to the top rather as petrol is squeezed into a cigarette lighter or oil will inevitably be spilled on the cabin floor. It is better to carry the side-lights on the cabin-top – in this position they can be more easily fixed and more easily seen. Although lower down than on the rigging, they are not so likely to be blown out or obscured by a sail. They are easier to fix in position, avoiding a walk up the deck in a rough sea carrying a lamp, to be fastened high up on the side-light screen outside the shrouds.

## Avoiding steamers

Good lights are even more essential for the single-hander than for manned yachts because a single-hander has to rely on the vigilance and good seamanship of others for his safety. The sure knowledge that he can be seen at night will contribute to his peace of mind and will make it easier for him to relax but he should not believe for a moment that because his boat carries good lights he will be safe. The only real safeguard against collision is his own alertness and good sense. If he himself can keep out of everyone's way he will be safe and he will cause no inconvenience to others – he should place the responsibility for his own safety firmly on his own shoulders. If a ship is seen approaching on a collision course it is, after all, a simple matter to keep clear regardless of who has the legal right of way. The farther she is away when she is first sighted, the smaller will be the alteration necessary to keep clear of her. Sometimes approach angles and speeds can be confusing and it is well worth it to reach in for the hand compass. If the bearing does not alter in a few minutes, action must be taken.

## Weather forecasts

Bad weather when coasting is many times more dangerous than bad weather in the open ocean. Sea room may be restricted, the seas may be rendered more destructive by a strong tidal stream, there may be shallow water in the offing and there is an added danger of being run down. The single-hander, along with every other yachtsman will be an addict for weather forecasts. Weather forecasts are invaluable in certain circumstances, but the single-hander should not allow them to rule his life. Of course no one should venture to sea in the teeth of gale warnings from a contrary direction, but at the same time a close watch should be kept on the barometer and the general weather signs.

An experienced yachtsman should use the weather forecast as a factor – albeit an important one – in his assessment of the weather situation. After all, he is the man on the spot and in some cases he may be a better judge. A forecaster, sits with his computer in some remote tower and gives local predictions based on facts which may be many hours old and which are applied to local areas by the use of a set of purely theoretical computations. If the man on the spot can see that it is a fine day with a steadily rising glass and fair wind he may decide to go to sea in spite of some dire prediction. It is not uncommon for a forecast to be accurate in content, but misplaced in time so that the predicted weather has already passed by. On the peripheries of forecast areas, a long way removed from the source, the information may be inaccurate. It is a commonplace to experience weather which is quite at odds with the forecast for days on end. These strictures apply to favourable as well as to unfavourable forecasts. There are cases where bad weather springs up suddenly to confound a favourable prediction and the single-hander must always watch his barometer and the local signs.

## Running for harbour

If he is "caught out" in bad weather near the coast the single-hander must think clearly and hard – should he make for harbour or should he see it through? If there is a good, safe port under his lee and the predictions, together with his own intelligence, tell him that a hard, unpleasant blow from the wrong direction is imminent, he will have no difficulty in deciding. Far better to be safely snugged down in some friendly harbour than flogging himself and his boat to pieces outside. But if the wind is fair for him the advantages of going in may be marginal. Harbours can be dangerous, difficult places to approach in worsening weather, more especially for a man by himself. Visibility may be bad, there may be a dangerous cross sea at the entrance or a strong, contrary tide. Once inside, he may find it hard to locate a safe berth – the harbour may be overcrowded with sheltering yachts and fishing boats, and he may be directed to moor in an unpleasant, exposed place. There may be a tidal basin inside which can only be entered or left at high tide which may entail a wait in a foul berth, to get in and again to get out. He may find himself tied against some concrete quay, or lying to his anchor in poor holding ground, or alongside a coaster or a fisherman in conditions of misery, with his topsides ground and scraped and seared and his beautiful white paint sullied with oil while a fine, abrasive grit is blown over his spotless decks from the quay. Then he will wish he was out in the honest ocean where at least he can be master of his own destiny.

## Keeping the sea

At sea, he may suffer a few hours' discomfort but more than likely his boat will be safe and he will be that much further on his way. The first essential is to gain sea room so that he cannot be caught on a lee shore. This may involve a considerable alteration of course but any extra distance to be sailed will be paid for by peace of mind. A yacht hove-to can make as much as two knots of leeway – an offing of at least twenty miles is desirable. Apart from the danger of a lee shore, the seas are likely to be smoother and more regular off shore, because there will be less tidal stream. If he is wise he will take the usual precautions for weathering a gale in good time. He will reef down until his boat is safe and riding easily and he will have his storm sails ready to bend on if the weather should deteriorate beyond what is usual for the season and the locality. In an increasing wind it is always better to tie in reefs before the need for them has become urgent, and thus keep the boat well within her capacity to cope with the strength of wind.

## Hard driving

If the wind is fair there is always the temptation to hang on to sail for too long in a rising gale, so that reefing, when it does become essential, is more difficult, even dangerous. In fact boats sail better and probably as fast if they are not carrying more sail than they need. This is especially true of the single-hander who will be relying on his vane gear for steering. Sooner or later, if it is subjected to undue strain, it will fail – possibly with serious consequences. Carrying too much sail in a strong wind makes hard work for a steering gear. If the wind is foul, there is much less temptation to carry too much sail owing to the sheer discomfort of beating to windward in a hard blow. With the wind fair a man is master of his boat and has the power to drive her as hard as he wishes – even to the point of destruction. In a contrary wind a well found yacht is master. She has more stamina to windward than any man by himself, and sooner or later the single-hander who fancies himself as a hard driver will be forced to shorten sail for the sake of his own nerve and his own comfort. There is the further consideration that the single-handed voyager is probably going a long way in a long time. He will be more interested in arriving at his destination with his boat and her gear intact than he is in making fast passages in bad weather. In bad weather he is at his weakest, because he is limited in everything he does by his own physical strength and because bad weather is wearing on the nerves and excessively tiring. He cannot afford the punishment to his own resources which comes inevitably from driving his boat too hard.

## The journal

By the time he passes the last cape and sets course across the ocean, leaving the land with its joys and its terrors finally and irrevocably behind him, he will have passed the first major test and weathered the first and possibly the most difficult part of his voyage. Now he can confide in his journal with a measure of satisfaction and a new found confidence. He can allow his truest and most private thoughts and feelings to spill over the pages in an uninhibited flood. The journal plays an important part in his psychological well-being, releasing for him all the pent up emotion and bottled feelings which he is unable otherwise to communicate. He will watch the dim, hazy line of the shore slide away behind him, taking with it the last fixed mark, the last authentic point of departure. He will experience a feeling of overwhelming humility – a sense of his own smallness and weakness and fragility when set against the momentous power of the ocean. From this moment on he is his own mentor, his own authority and his own judge. His bedfellow is the ocean whose moods and whims he must understand and accommodate himself to, offering to the Gods his brains, his intelligence and his meagre strength and trusting that they will look favourably upon his enterprise.

# 5 BASIC INSTRUMENTS AND THEIR USE

A sailing boat is essentially a simple mechanism run on changeless principles. The single-hander would be well advised to keep it this way. The instruments which he needs to conduct his voyage are also, essentially, simple and they are very few. Each one of them is of vital importance – they must be guarded and cherished. Barometer, compass, sextant, chronometer, radio, log, can be marked as essentials with the echo sounder as a close contender. A tape recorder is an invaluable instrument to have on board. Every vessel will have more than one compass on board, the chronometer, or deck watch, can be doubled with a wrist watch, there should be two radios, one a direction finder, two sextants if possible or at least spare sextant mirrors and several spare log lines and rotators. By losing or damaging any one of his essential instruments the single-hander will be seriously inconvenienced. Many voyages have been successfully completed without instruments, but no single-hander will have peace of mind unless he can find his way across the oceans and around the coast lines with certitude.

## The barometer

An understanding of the significance of a barometer and the ability to read its message are of vital importance to a single-handers wellbeing. Without a compass, a good estimate of direction can always be made from observing the sun and the stars, just as a position can be estimated without sextant, chronometer or log often with remarkable accuracy. But there is no way of estimating atmospheric pressure without a barometer and changes of pressure are the basic cause of all weather change. Barometric readings must be entered in the log frequently – at least every two hours – so that a continuous pattern of readings can be built up, or better still, the single-hander should carry a barograph, which will give a complete picture at a glance. The lone sailor, above all else, is vulnerable to the vagaries of the weather. The barometer offers him the means of arming himself in advance against his most dreaded enemy. He must be, in the last analysis, his own weather forecaster and for this task the barometer is his only tool. Coupled with his ability to read the visual signals which the weather usually sends out in advance, the barometer gives him the means to make a shrewd estimate of danger, or a confident forecast of fair weather. In my view the barometer is the most important instrument of all.

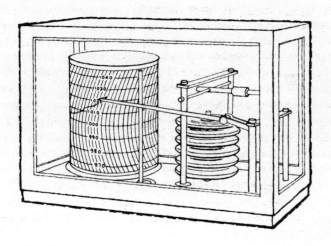

*Barograph. Best instrument for noting changes in atmospheric pressure.*

## The compass

The instrument which is fundamental to voyaging by sea is the mariner's compass: it is critical to his personal success or failure as a navigator. It must be his constant preoccupation to keep his boat on course. In a crewed yacht the compass is watched throughout the day and night by the man at the wheel, but the single-hander has other preoccupations. He must arrange it, as far as possible, so that the compass is within his view by day and by night. The master compass, or standard compass, on which the course is set should be positioned on the centre line of the yacht where it can readily be seen from above and from all sides as well as from the steering position. This compass must be swung before the voyage starts and a deviation card made out either by the single-hander himself or by a compass adjuster. In a wooden or a fibreglass boat it should not be difficult to install a compass which has no deviation to speak of, but in a steel or even a concrete boat with steel reinforcement, it might be necessary to have the boat swung by a professional.

In addition to the standard compass there must be at least one compass inside the boat which can be moved from one position to another so that it is always within view. A grid compass of at least six inches diameter with a luminous, adjustable ring which can be lined up with the course is ideal for this purpose. The compass should be of the type that can be clipped into a socket which is fastened to the bulkhead or any vertical surface. Several sockets should be positioned round the cabin so that the compass can easily and quickly be moved from one to the other at will. Each time it is moved the grid is re-set to the course from the standard compass so that no account need be taken of deviation or error in the cabin compass. There should be a position in the centre of the cabin, one by each bunk and other positions as convenient so that, in one position or another, the compass can always be seen.

Before sleep, the single-hander should position the compass by his bunk. If he should be woken by some change in the yacht's motion or an unusual or unfamiliar hesitation in her pace he can first open one eye and check that he is on course

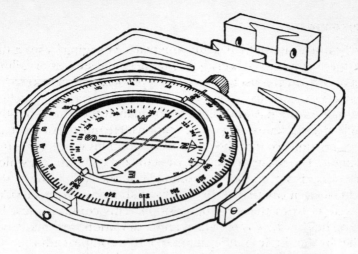

*Grid compass positioned inside yacht for checking course at any time. Several sockets can be installed, provided deviation is checked at each position.*

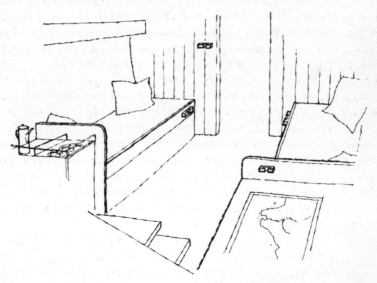

*Where the grid compass may be clipped on.*

61

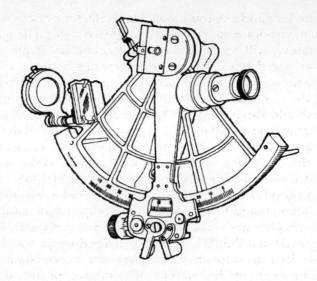

*His most prized possession.*

before deciding whether she needs his attention. Without this simple device the yacht can stray off course undetected for long periods, upsetting the DR position, threatening the accuracy of his navigation and adding unnecessary miles to the distance run. In a short time the single-hander will find that he is constantly aware of the ship's head, at least during his hours awake.

## The chronometer

Apart from sunset and sunrise, the demands of navigation will make arbitrary divisions in the single-hander's day over which he has little control. If he navigates by the sun, which is the simplest and most reliable method of finding a position at sea, he must take his sights at approximately the same time each day, either during the forenoon or the afternoon and, in addition, a meridian altitude at noon. He must have a chronometer or a watch to give him GMT, which is necessary in order to compute longitude. A traditional chronometer or deck watch, which incorporates a device to compensate for changes in temperature, will have a steady and constant daily rate which must be logged in a special chronometer rate book. In spite of being temperature compensated for changes between day and night, the rate may vary slightly with the overall temperature which should also be logged. The instrument should be checked at the same time each day from a radio time signal and the daily rate marked down. If because of radio interference or any other cause the daily time check cannot be made, GMT can be calculated without difficulty from this chronometer log.

With a good radio, time checks should be available in any part of the ocean, but radios, susceptible to damp and all manner of defects, may become unusable on a long voyage. A quartz watch can be used but it should be carefully watched and checked daily because its rate, though small, may not be constant. The chronometer should be kept in a safe, dry place protected from damp and sudden movement. It should be placed where it does not have to be moved when used perhaps in a drawer or a small locker close to the chart table or in a box with a glass lid. It must be wound at the same time each day and its error entered in the book under five headings. 1. Date. 2. ST (ship's time), 3. +/−", 4. Daily rate, 5. Temperature.

## The sextant

The most august occupant of the dry, safe space near the chart table must be the single-hander's sextant, surely his most prized possession. A navigator will treasure his sextant for as long as he follows the sea – it is the symbol of his craft. He becomes used to the feel of his own instrument and will be at home with no other. A navigator in a small yacht, particularly if he is alone, must place absolute reliance in his sextant because without it he is a blind man. It is the actual taking of a sight, from an unstable, low-down position on the deck of a small yacht, that is crucial to the success of his navigation. The sextant is always at risk and is vulnerable to damage. It must be guarded and preserved against accident with the utmost care.

Since its invention in 1757 the sextant has not changed in principle – any instrument made since that time is perfectly usuable today. The only significant advance has been the micrometer scale in place of a vernier, which vastly simplifies the reading of the angle. Sextants made from plastic material are less expensive than the traditional instrument and in some cases are excellent, although not generally as accurate or as pleasant to use. They have the advantage of being lighter but because the material is to some extent volatile they suffer a loss of accuracy from changes of temperature.

The most vulnerable components of any sextant are the index and horizon mirrors because the silvered coating on these mirrors is susceptible to salt corrosion. They must be carefully

*Sextant mirror which has been allowed to become corroded.*

wiped with a chamois cloth without fail every time the sextant is used and if the instrument is inadvertently doused in spray, the mirrors must be dismantled, cleaned with warm, fresh water and thoroughly dried out. Once corrosion sets in it will spread day by day across the mirror and there is no way of stopping it. After a period of time the mirror and thereby the sextant itself, will become useless. There is no way of arresting mirror corrosion once it has taken hold although it may spread across the mirror at varying speeds depending on the seriousness of the taint. For this reason it is an obvious precaution to carry spare mirrors, suitably smothered in vaseline.

Apart from mirrors, the sextant is easily damaged unless great care is taken and against this risk the only security is to have a second sextant on board, perhaps a less expensive plastic instrument. It is not easy to get mirrors re-silvered in many foreign parts, let alone a repair to the sextant itself. The arc and the tangent screw should be kept lubricated with the fine vegetable oil that is normally supplied with the instrument and all moisture should be wiped away from the shades. It may suffer from salt corrosion when not in use for long periods. It should be taken out of its box every so often for an airing and a drop of oil.

Sextant lore is riddled with ancient tradition which should be taken note of because, as with most tradition, it is founded on good sense. There is a correct way of taking the sextant out of its box. The box should be placed where it cannot slide with the yacht's motion and where there is space for the lid to be fully opened. When the sextant is in the box the index bar should be positioned at approximately thirty degrees so that the tangent screw will clear the sides of the box. The instrument should then be lifted at the centre of the frame with the left hand and transferred to the right hand where it should be held by the handle only. The silvered arc of a vernier sextant should not be touched by the fingers.

### Taking a sight

When a sight is to be taken, the sextant must be carried on deck without being knocked and taken to the chosen position which should be as high above the level of the sea as possible. Taking an accurate sight from the deck of a yacht is a precarious and highly skilled business that takes time and patience and judgement to master. It is the most difficult part of yacht navigation on which accuracy depends absolutely. Having no one to take the time for him, the single-hander should carry a stop watch on a line round his neck. He should be wearing the safety harness and he should be chocked against the mast or the boom gallows, or even a stay, so that he can have both hands free for the sextant without losing balance. He should pre-set the approximate altitude on the instrument and then sweep the horizon until he finds the sun, rather than bring the sun down to the horizon which entails an additional feat of balance.

The art of the business is to position the sun on the actual horizon and not on a wave or the ridge or a long swell which may look very like the horizon. Having a height of eye which is unlikely to be greater than 8 ft and working from a platform which may be oscillating violently it is not easy to take an accurate altitude. The secret is to be relaxed and to be so securely chocked or fastened that concentration can be wholly focussed on the sextant. The single-hander must fix on an instant when the sun is at the exact bottom of the sextant's swing and when it is balanced on a clear segment of horizon and with his left hand, press the button of the stop-watch. He must then make his way as quickly as possible back to the chronometer or deck watch, take the time and apply the stop watch reading to it.

He should remember that every time he takes a sight the sextant is at risk and therefore the greatest care must be taken. Everything must be ready beforehand including a pad and pencil. The motion of a yacht in the ocean is always heavy, even in calm, settled weather. When it is rough and the yacht is sailing hard the motion is violent. The steady roll which the single-hander becomes quite accustomed to is then overlaid by leaps and lurches and jerks as she forces her way at speed through and across the uneven lumps of ocean. It may be impossible to gain a clear vision of both the sun and the horizon because the sails are interposed except in some unacceptable position for taking a sight such as the lee side-deck for'ard. In this case the yacht must be settled on a new course while sights are being taken. Running before the trades the yacht will roll through an arc of thirty or forty degrees every three seconds. It is an easy thing to trip or lose balance and even drop or knock the sextant or to allow it to get wet with spray, any of which might be disastrous.

*Single-hander must be secured when taking astro sights, leaving both hands free for the sextant.*

It will be seen that taking a sight is a feat of dexterity worthy of a circus acrobat – it is one of the operations at sea which is many times more difficult for a single-hander. A companion would pass the sextant to him when he is already in position to take the sight, would mark the time in response to a shout and would trim the yacht on a course to bring the sails clear of the sun and the horizon. It is usual to take more than one sight and then to average out the times and the altitudes or to work two sights side by side taking a mean of the result.

## Daily sights essential

On a long passage in the ocean the single-hander may consider it unnecessary to take sights every day. He may decide to work on DR and to wait until he is approaching a landfall – perhaps two or three days out – before fixing his position, or he may think that he can use his DR until he nears the land and then pick up a radio bearing which will guide him in. A surprising number of single-handers are prone to this habit – most seamen would agree that it is bad practise and for a single-hander, doubly so. A navigator's religion is to know his position at all times as nearly as is practicable. The man who trusts his way across the ocean in the belief that he can pick up his position in good time may be disappointed. He may find that the sun and the stars decide to take a holiday for a few days behind clouds, just when he wants them. He may find that the radio beacon is out of service or that his own receiver has succumbed to the damp salt air. Errors in DR can be and usually are cumulative, one day's mistake or misjudgement compounding that of the next. The habit of taking sights and fixing the position every day, even if it seems pointless in the vast spaces of the ocean where a few miles one way or the other are irrelevant, is a good one. Psychologically, it helps the single-hander – he can compete with himself from one day's run to the next, he can see the indisputable proof that his voyage across the infinity of ocean is progressing, albeit slowly.

A good navigator will learn more about the performance of his boat every day so that when necessary he is better positioned to estimate his DR and above all, his mastery of the art of finding his way across the oceans will give him confidence and the firm conviction that he is in all respects the master of his craft. The art of navigation is an unending fascination with subtle variants and surprising innovations available to he who seeks them out. The practice and constant performance of the art on a long sea passage will serve to make the navigator more aware of the complex beauty and completeness which exists in the order which surrounds him and which in turn allows him to exist.

## Star sights

The stars and the moon are of less every day value to the single-handed navigator than the sun, although at times they are invaluable. In fine, clear weather when the boat is reasonably stable star sights at morning or evening are practicable. They can often give a welcome fix before a night landfall, perhaps on an unlit shore, or a quick check on latitude from the Pole Star can be useful. They have the advantage, unlike the sun, of giving a fixed position from one set of sights. But in rough seas when the boat is lively, to identify a pair of stars, to fix them in the sextant's mirror and accurately to bring them down to the horizon and time them, is fiend's work. A quick sight of the sun on the other hand, snatched between scudding cloud when the boat is shaking and twisting in the seas, can give an accurate result when it would be impossible to catch a star in the sextant's mirror for more than an instant.

## Venus on the meridian

None the less, star navigation has many surprises and happy chances to offer the lone sailor. For instance, it is sometimes possible to take a latitude by Meridian Altitude of the planet Venus in the forenoon or the afternoon when it can be observed in the sextant's star telescope if the approximate altitude is preset. This can be combined with a longitude by chronometer of the sun to produce an excellent position – perhaps as exact a position as is possible in a small yacht.

The moon also offers boundless opportunities to the adventurous navigator although it is little used nowadays. Captain Slocum was a lunarian and was able to calculate his longitude with no better chronometer than his famous one-handed alarm clock.

## Longitude without chronometer

It is possible to calculate longitude by the sun without a chronometer and without nautical tables by a delightfully

69

simple method which is seldom given in navigation books and is not widely used. A sight is taken in the forenoon and the time is taken with a wrist watch or clock. At noon a latitude by Meridian Altitude is calculated and in the afternoon another sight is taken when the sun is at the same altitude as the morning sight, plus or minus a correction for any difference in the latitude between the sights. The two times are added together and divided by 2 to give a mean and the sun's GHA at that time taken from the Almanac, is the longitude (example). As a guide, the first sight should be taken at least as many minutes before estimated noon as there are degrees in the latitude.

## Example

On May 24th, 1975, in DR Lat. 38° 53′ N. and DR Lon. 30° 41′ W. the time of noon was calculated as 1359 GMT. A sight of the sun was taken at 1318 GMT. Course 094° (T).

| | | | | |
|---|---|---|---|---|
| 1st sight | 1318 GMT | Watch reading 13h 20m 29s | | Sextant reading 69° 33′ |
| 2nd sight | 1340 GMT | Watch reading 14 42 37 | | Sextant reading 69° 33′ |

$$\begin{array}{r} 2)\overline{28 \quad 03 \quad 06} \\ 14 \quad 01 \quad 33 \end{array}$$

watch error     − 02 39

$$\begin{array}{r} \overline{13 \quad 58 \quad 54} \\ 00° \quad 49.1′ \\ 29 \quad 30.0 \\ 13.5 \end{array}$$

GHA     30° 32.6′ = Longitude

*Meridian Altitude*

| | | |
|---|---|---|
| Obs Alt. | 71° | 37′ |
| Corr. | | + 13 |
| (T) alt. | 71 | 50 |
| | 90 | 00 |
| ZD | 18 | 10 |
| Dec | 20 | 43N |
| Lat. | 38 | 53N |

*Observed noon position*

| | | |
|---|---|---|
| Lat. | 38° | 53′N |
| Lon. | 30 | 32½W |

If the yacht's course had been in a northerly or southerly direction sufficient to change her latitude between the two sights, it would have been necessary to change the sextant angle for the second sight by the number of minutes of change of latitude. The reading would be increased if the latitude change was towards the sun and vice versa.

## Radio direction finding

Navigation by radio is something of an art and some of the equipment available to a yachtsman is highly sophisticated. However, marine radio bearings are not difficult to pick up on any radio. They are found in the long wave band. The best radio direction finders for the single-hander are those which incorporate a compass so that the bearing can be read off direct from the instrument regardless of whether the yacht is exactly on course or not. An error of less than five degrees should not be relied on, as the null from a radio beacon may cover a span of as much as fifteen degrees so that the actual bearing may be no more than an estimate. For this reason, cross bearings of three or more beacons are often unsatisfactory.

Aircraft beacons, provided they are situated on the coast so that the bearing does not travel across the land, are often of more use to the single-hander than marine beacons because they transmit a continuous signal; he does not have to wait for the sequence and in consequence they are easier to pick up. The difficulty here is that they may not be listed in nautical publications. Sometimes air radio beacons are all that are available, but they are notoriously fickle and should not be relied on to identify a landfall. They can be invaluable for "homing" in thick weather when suitably placed. If the DF set is coupled to a loudspeaker, a single-hander can steer and keep a look out and listen, at the same time as he keeps his ship's head in the null. Care should be taken that the correct bearing is not the reciprocal – sometimes an easy mistake – and that the signal does not come across the land, which may distort its direction. Bearings can also be distorted at sun-set and sun-rise.

As a fall-back, most portable radios have built-in directional

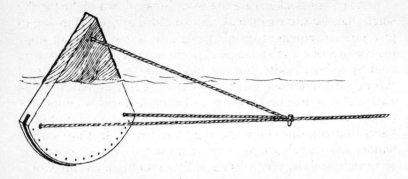

*Wooden ship log: use it if all your patent logs are eaten by sharks.*

aerials and can be used as direction finders simply by swinging the set until the null is obtained the bearing being noted on the standard compass. Care should be taken not to position the radio close to the compass as this can cause a substantial error.

## The log

Modern yachts are usually fitted with bottom logs which protrude through the hull and are operated by small impellers, but many single-handers still use the traditional Walker patent log, which has remained much the same since 1884 when it was perfected by Thomas Walker. The instrument is hard-wearing and accurate although in the ocean the rotators are sometimes taken by sharks or other large fish particularly in a calm when the log line may hang vertically downwards. In these circumstances the line should be taken on board until the breeze springs up again. The rotators sometimes foul with weed and should be inspected every few days or if sights show the measurements to be inaccurate. The synthetic log lines that are now supplied seem to be stronger and better wearing than fibre lines. Spare lines and rotators should be carried. A remarkable degree of accuracy may be found when the log distance is compared with actual distance at the end of an ocean passage.

As a last fall-back in case of loss or break-down of the log the single-hander can easily make up an old fashioned ship-log to give a measurement of speed through the water. A proper ship-log consists of a small triangle of wood, weighted at one side and held by a short bridle, but any object that does not easily pull through the water will do, such as an old cushion soaked in sea water. This is dropped over on a line marked with a knot every twenty-five feet and is timed for fifteen seconds, the number of knots that run out being the yacht's speed. In fact the single-hander will soon learn to estimate his speed through the water accurately and to make a very good guess at his day's run. Comparing the guess with reality is useful and interesting diversion.

## Hand lead

It is worth carrying a properly marked lead line, kept available in one of the cockpit lockers, in case of an echo sounder break-down. Heaving the lead is a particularly

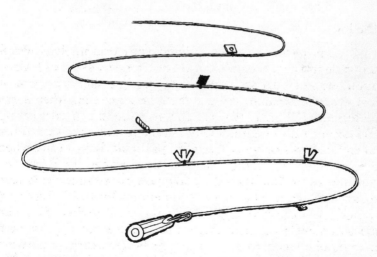

*This is a traditional hand lead line — in case you have never seen one!*

tiresome occupation for a single-hander because it consumes his time at the very moment he has other, pressing things to be doing – in shallows or coming up to an anchorage or entering harbour. But the hand lead still has qualities that the echo sounder lacks and it should not be disdained as a piece of yacht equipment. It has the virtue of accuracy and reliability and, unlike the sounder, it can tell the single-hander something of the quality of the bottom – whether it is sand or shingle or mud, hard or soft, rocky or even. This may be useful in fog to check a position from the chart datum, or in coming up to anchor. The lead can be "armed" with heavy grease (tallow is a thing of the past) so that it will bring up a sample of the bottom – a dodge as old as the sea itself and not to be despised. The best way of marking the hand lead line is still by the traditional method, because the depths can be read off in the dark, by feel.

| 1 fathom | A piece of twine with one knot, |
| 2 fathoms | A piece of leather with 2 ends |
| 3 fathoms | A piece of leather with 3 ends |
| 5 fathoms | A piece of white terylene |
| 7 fathoms | A piece red flag bunting |
| 10 fathoms | A piece of square leather with a hole in it |

## Tape-recorder

A small tape-recorder can be coupled to the ship's radio, which is likely to have a bigger and better loudspeaker and will therefore give better reproduction. It is a delightful instrument for a single-hander to carry and will give him infinite pleasure as well as being of great practical use. Weather forecasts can be taped if they come through at inconvenient moments and can be listened to and digested later. A selection of music can be brought from home and this can be added to with taped broadcasts from local radio stations. The sounds of the ocean and of the yacht herself – the noise of a gale and the noise of a calm, a wild bird or the throaty breathing of dolphins as they leap through the waves, singing and carousals in the cabin in foreign ports – can all be listened to nostalgically when the voyage is over and may give an interesting record of events in sound. The tapes are susceptible to damp and should be stowed in a box with silicon bags. Short play tapes C 60's and C 90's are most suitable – C 120 tapes are easily tangled and have little tolerance to damp. A lead made up with plugs on each end should be carried so that tapes can be copied from other yachts.

There is a wide variety of instruments in use on modern yachts with dials and lights and flickering needles enough to confuse a senior wrangler. But few, if any, of them are of much practical use to the single-hander. He will be voyaging far away from his base where the servicing and replacement of "gadgets" will be difficult and expensive. He will, if he is wise, place his faith in the well tried tools of his calling which have been proven over the generations of mariners. These he will learn to respect and trust and interpret sensibly and correctly and he will find them sufficient to carry him in confidence to the furthest corners of the world. Anything in excess is no more than a conceit which may cause him trouble and expense, but which will not contribute to the good management of his voyage.

# 6  ACCIDENTS AND AILMENTS

A yacht at sea, running before the boisterous trades with her twins set and the ocean chuckling under her bow, is like a thoroughbred horse – highly strung, tense, unpredicatable. She will roll through thirty or forty degrees every three or four seconds, but as often as not she will vary her gait with a sudden pause or a hurried change of step or an unexpected and contrary plunge or lurch in some rogue direction. To the single-hander her motion becomes his own second nature. He learns to adjust his own balance to the inconsistencies of her motion, subconsciously matching his own adjustments of sway and swing in response to her dictates. The ensuing dance, which would appear ludicrous if it could be observed out of the context of the ocean which causes it, is the single-hander's greatest hazard and also the greatest contributor towards his well-being. On a long passage the yacht's constant and more or less violent motion gives him the exercise which is essential to his good health. It also makes him vulnerable to injury from a dangerous fall.

Life on board a yacht would be an enervating affair without the motion, comparable to being locked up in a small room for a month at a time. Apart from physical jerks and artificial exercises a man living ashore in the ordinary course of life gets enough physical movement in his daily round to keep himself, if not fit, at least tolerably well. This natural exercise is normally enough although he may wish to supplement it for the sake of his general physical well-being by cycling or trotting or playing a game or some form of gymnastics. The single-hander needs none of this. His exercise is provided for him all day and all night by the constant use of every muscle in his body in order to keep his balance and maintain himself, when standing, in a vertical posture. For every second of the day, even when he is asleep, he will be adjusting and countering and bracing himself against the incessant movement of the ship. This exercise is in addition to the physical work a single-hander will have to perform in order to keep his boat running.

If he still feels short of exercise there are many ways in which he can get it in a perfectly natural manner. He can form the habit of swinging himself down into the cabin by his arms each time he comes in from the cockpit, or he can turn the engine with the starting handle every day in order to keep it and himself loose, or he can climb a short way up the mast each evening to get a long view of the horizon. He will find at the end of an Atlantic crossing for example that he has lost weight and that his muscles, in the legs, arms and stomach are hard and supple. He will also find that he has a tremedous appetite and will probably eat more than he does ashore.

**General fitness**

For some hours or even days when he comes ashore after a long passage he will find it difficult to adapt. When he stands on "terra firma", it will, for him, continue to sway and roll until he has adjusted. For several days he will find, when he stands still in some office or drawing-room, that his stance will be with the legs wide apart and feet firmly placed on the ground, bracing himself against an imaginary roll. He may suffer from vertigo when he first comes ashore and this may last for several days. He may experience some difficulty in communicating – he may suffer from a deep sense of loneliness which he never experienced alone on board his boat, because he finds it difficult to make contact with other human beings.

Keeping himself healthy and free from illness and injury is vital to the lone sailor – there will be no respite for him, no other person to look after him and sympathize with him if he falls ill or injures himself at sea. He will be helped by his surroundings and his general way of life. He will get more exercise in a day than he would be likely to take in a week at home and he will get the food he is used to. He will always drink the same water which, if he has been provident, he knows to be pure and good. He may, it is true, suffer from some fundamental malaise such as heart disease, which would be unlikely to have anything to do with being alone at sea.

### The right food

Diet is fundamental to good health at sea, as it is ashore. Whatever may be his way of life – vegetarianism, veganism, a high protein diet with heavy meat eating or, as is most common, a mixed diet, can be continued at sea. His state of health should be improved. He will be free from contagious diseases and largely free from infections. He can take on board fresh vegatables and fruit and cheese and eggs to last him a month or more if he is provident in what he buys and how he stows it. His meat and fish will be provided from tins and he should have no difficulty in getting the calories he needs for an energetic life and the protein he needs for a good balance. He may supplement his diet with fresh fish if he is lucky or skilful. He may suffer some vitamin deficiencies from time to time depending to some extent on where he obtains his supplies but this can be guarded against by carrying a supply of vitamin tablets. These can either be bought as individual vitamins or in composite form with a balanced mixture of all the vitamins he needs. If he begins to feel run-down and out of sorts for no particular reason, vitamin deficiency may well be his trouble. Vitamin C tablets in effervescent form are pleasant to take and are readily absorbed by the body.

### Medical check

Before leaving home it is prudent to have a medical check – a doctor may uncover some physical weakness which, even if it does not hazard the whole project, could put the single-hander on guard. He should check that he has the necessary immunizations for each country he visits – it may be wise to take some inoculations, even if they are not legally required. A person coming from a country where diseases such as polio are unknown or rare, may be more at risk than the locals in a country where they are prevalent. Hot climates have their own health problems – malaria perhaps or dysentery on which a friendly doctor will offer his advice before the voyage begins. The doctor could also be asked to prescribe a general antibiotic which is likely to be effective for most contingencies.

## Infections

Most important is never to set off on a voyage if he is unwell in the expectation that the symptons will pass away as soon as he is clear of the harbour – the opposite may well happen. Then he may find himself in need of care and medical attention and perhaps incapacitated at the very moment when he must have all his physical resources about him.

A small cut may become slightly infected before he leaves harbour and the single-hander may treat it lightly at the time and decide to leave as planned. It may get worse, quite slowly day by day, until he finds himself with a fully poisoned hand or foot or finger after he has been at sea for a week with an ocean under his lee. In these circumstances he may need to carry out an operation on himself. If the condition does not respond to any medicaments he has with him such as antibiotics or penicillin and if the infected part continues to get steadily more painful and more swollen day by day and to spread so that it renders him unable to work the ship, he may have to make an incision into the arm, leg or finger in order to let poison out.

## Limitations of pain killers

He is likely to recognize when this becomes necessary because the poisoned member will be so swollen and tender and the pain so intense and obviously getting worse, that it is quite impossible for him to carry on without taking some action. Unless he is able to use an anaesthetic which will act only locally on the part affected, the single-hander will have to perform an operation unaided by any pain killer. A general analgesic such as morphine will also affect his own ability to perform the operation. However, in extreme conditions of pain, a level of desperation is reached when any action, however drastic and unpleasant, is preferable to the continuous, nagging and incapacitating effect of a poisoned limb.

## Likelihood of injury

As most everday illnesses are spread in one way or another by contact with other people, the single-hander is likely to be free of them. If he looks after himself with reasonable care he will find that his way of living, with healthy activity, exercise, fresh air, regular meals and rest and a calm and contented outlook on life, is conducive to excellent health. However, he may easily suffer an accident – in fact, he will be lucky on a long voyage if he does not. Living with the motion generated by a small yacht goes a long way towards keeping the single-hander well but sooner or later the same motion is likely to cause him to fall heavily and break a bone, crack a rib or receive a hard knock on the head resulting in concussion. Or he may cut himself or burn and scald himself with boiling water or boiling soup. It is worth taking a few simple precautions against this likelihood of injury.

## Precautions

Hard corners of wood or metal in the cabin should be covered with some cushioning material such as foam rubber. This can be fixed with an adhesive along the edges of the inside of the coach-roof and on any other potentially dangerous protuberances in the cabin. The galley, which is perhaps the primary source of danger, should be arranged in such a way that the single-hander can sit down, securely wedged in position and at the same time reach the essential utensils. It should not be necessary at any time to lean over the stove in such a way that clothing can catch alight. Positions should be arranged where hot saucepans can be put down where they cannot spill or fall with the motion of the ship.

An obvious precaution against a fall is to wear shoes that do not slip either on deck or in the cabin, or better still to get used to wearing no shoes. Shoes of any kind are an encumbrance on a boat except for warmth in exceptionally cold weather. They serve no useful purpose but they require valuable time to be put on and taken off. They encourage clumsiness and they are invariably slippery in wet conditions. Unless they are made of canvas and rope they tend to make the feet hot and uncomfortable. A man who gets used to being on board without shoes will learn to tread carefully, even daintily on board and he will learn very quickly to avoid banging and hurting his feet. His feet will get tough and his toes will straighten as he uses them unfettered by shoes, to aid his balance, which, after all, is their purpose. In the days of square rig, sailors never wore shoes.

## Essential books

A proper first aid kit and a good first aid manual are both indispensable. The *Authorized Manual of the Red Cross Society* is a publication which should be carried by all yachts. It is easy to follow, amply illustrated and contains information on every aspect of first aid and common illness. Another informative and clearly written manual is the *International Medical Guide for Ships*, written for ship's captains who sail without a doctor on board. This is an excellent volume full of information and readily understandable. It is comprehensive enough to be used by a doctor and at the same time can be understood by a layman.

## The first aid kit

Lists of essential first aid materials and medicines can be obtained from many sources. A kit purchased from a good-class chemist can be a basis which the single-hander can build on according to his knowledge and his preference – what he takes with him and leaves behind from the inexhaustible choice of first aid gear must be a matter for his own common sense. Crepe bandages are better and firmer than cotton for putting on splints or for keeping a dressing in place or bandaging a sprain – they can also be washed. Triangular bandages should also be carried. Adhesive dressing strips can be bought in varying sizes or in a continuous roll to be cut as required. There should be plenty of cotton wool but in small packs rather than large, a superfluity of safety pins, surgical scissors having one pointed blade and one blunt (for removing stitches). It is worth having two pairs of scissors in the first aid kit – sooner or later one is likely to be taken for the bos'n's box or the galley.

### The three B's

A splinter forceps can double as a dressing forceps, a tourniquet can be a piece of rubber tubing. Sutures for joining a wound should be carried on board – Dumbell sutures can take the place of sticking plaster and unless a cut is very deep can be used in place of stitches. For very large cuts pre-sterilized sutures sealed in a glass tube with needles and thread and instructions for use all in one packet should be included in the first aid box. An eye dropper can double as a filler to remove compass bubbles, a hot-water bottle as a chock for noisy bottles, an old glove as finger stalls – a most important item. Bites and stings can be unpleasant and should be treated with bicarbonate of soda after the sting has been removed. Insect repellent to rub on exposed parts of the body and insecticide for the cabin may make the difference between comfort and misery. The yacht's cabin should have gauze covers for the hatches which let in air but not insects. The three commonest causes of distress are the three B's – burns, breaks and bleeding. The first aid locker should provide at least some measure of relief from all of them.

### Emergency operation

No single-hander will perform an operation on himself unless it is clear beyond doubt that some extreme action must be taken because of an infection which will respond to no other treatment. The essentials are to have everything ready to hand before the operation starts, to sterilize every instrument that is to be used, to have plenty of hot water ready, not boiling, and a good supply of bandage, towels, cottonwool, a plastic bucket and some diluted disinfectant, such as Dettol. It is wise to have a tot of spirit ready in a glass to take after the operation or during it if necessary to avoid fainting.

If a scalpel is used it must be sharp, or failing this a stainless steel safety-razor blade in a holder is adequate. The manual gives instructions for sterilization. He must decide carefully where the incision is to be made and when everything is prepared he should make, if possible, a single deep cut into the poisoned part being careful to avoid cutting an artery. Pus will immediately be released – the wound should be lightly pressed to evacuate it properly and then dressed with a suture according to the manual.

## Dressings

To know how to dress a wound is very important for the single-handed sailor – if he gets an infection he may be in serious trouble. He ought to understand the basic sterile techniques for dressing a wound which can be found in the ship's guide or the first aid manual and which should be studied before rather than after the emergency has arisen. It is possible to buy a pack of spray-on wound dressing – this is now employed in hospitals. Provided the wound is not too large a spray-on dressing will cover it with a thin but tough film which at the same time as being quick and simple to use will give immediate protection against infection. It has the added advantage of allowing the wound to "breathe" naturally. These dressings should be carried by a single-hander for the treatment of small wounds.

## Concussion

If he should miss his balance, fall heavily and crack his head against some solid object so as to knock himself out, or slip on deck and fall headlong into the cockpit, banging his head against a hard wooden seat or some metal fitting, a single-hander may find himself lying unconscious on the deck or cabin sole. On regaining consciousness he should, without any delay, get himself down into the cabin and installed in a comfortable position. He should do this at once, because in the first minutes he regains consciousness after a knock-out his brain will be clear and any damage he has sustained, unless it is very serious, will not immediately make itself apparent. This is because after a period of unconsciousness, blood rushes back to the brain with renewed vigour and the heart, for a short time pumps up the circulation to a higher than normal rate. After a few minutes this will settle itself down and an injury, such as a concussion will make itself felt.

The only way the single-hander can treat a concussion is to lie in a comfortable position and stay still and quiet. He will have to leave his boat to her own devices while he rests until the effects of the concussion pass off, eating nothing and drinking nothing but a little water. He should not lie on his back – he may vomit and in this position, if he is unconscious or semi-conscious, the vomit will be drawn into the lungs which may be fatal. Unless it is serious, in which case it will need medical attention which is not available, a mild concussion will probably pass away in a few hours or, at worst in a day or so. It may leave him with more or less serious headaches for a period of time, but this too will, in time, pass off.

## Broken bones

A bad fall in a heavy seaway when the boat is moving violently can easily result in a fractured bone – a very serious injury for a man by himself. Broken fingers, arms, or even legs are a serious possibility and the single-hander should make some provision for such an accident. He should have in his first aid locker a variety of ready cut splints suitable for any bone which is likely to be fractured, particularly the fingers which are most at risk. Provided he has splints already cut – they should be padded with cotton wool if they are not comfortable – and plenty of rolled bandage it should be possible to set a simple fracture if it is not multiple or compound. The limb must be immobilized as quickly as possible. In a simple fracture the bone is cracked or broken and the tissues around it are not involved. Splints can be temporarily held in position with sticking plaster or tape, the bone set in position as nearly as possible and the bandage wound round as tightly as will not impede the flow of blood. It is also good sense to carry on board strong elastic braces for the wrists, arms and ankles. In the case of a serious injury such as compound fracture where the bone may be protruding through the skin, there is nothing much the single-hander can do but try to pull the injury into the best shape possible, immobilize the limb and set course, if he is able, for the nearest harbour or shipping route and call for help. Once a break of that nature sets in the wrong position it is likely to result in a serious and permanent disability.

**Toothache**

Perhaps the most traumatic malady to be borne on a long voyage alone is toothache. The single-hander should visit a dentist before he leaves home and have a thorough check, explaining his intention to the dentist so that no dubiously repaired cavity or active decay is left unattended. He should take on board a pain killer which can be painted on the teeth – oil of cloves is a natural ameliorator of pain which is effective and superior to a drug which will impair the single-hander's capacity to handle the ship. He should have on board a dentist's mirror and a proper dentist's probe, an instrument which is made of hard stainless steel and which is designed to dig out the inside of a cavity and to clean away a broken tooth. Filling cement can be used by a man on his own teeth and can often cover a nerve and relieve pain until help can be reached. Alternatively a filling which comes out intact or the piece of a broken tooth can be refastened with two-part glue as a temporary measure.

Toothache can drive a man alone insane, the relentless pain worrying away at the balance of his sanity. Self-extractions are almost impossible unless the tooth is already loose. Lone sailors have been known to fasten nylon twine to an infected tooth and to pull and jerk against the anchored end, but this device usually succeeds only in cutting the gum or cheek or breaking the twine. A certain relief can be experienced after such an attempt when the extra pain which it caused finally ceases.

## Tropical sun

The lone sailor is not likely to suffer from such things as heat stroke and tummy upsets because his introduction to climatic change is gradual and because he carries his own water and food on board. However, he can easily experience headaches from glare reflected from water and white sails – he should be provided with several pairs of good quality sunglasses. Tanned or coloured sails are a relief from excessive glare.

In tropical harbours sun awnings are essential for the health of the lone sailor and for the preservation of his ship – they must be a part of the equipment of a yacht sailing to tropical shores. They should be wide enough to shade the whole boat and if they cannot be made to extend well out over each side, they should have flaps which drop downwards. Good awnings made from an opaque material make the difference between happiness and extreme discomfort in the tropics. The undiluted rays of the overhead sun when at anchor in a sheltered harbour are insupportable to man and boat without protection. Even at sea it is often wise to rig a small awning over the cockpit if this is practicable. It is wise to take salt tablets every day in the tropics to compensate for the salt lost through perspiration.

## Swimming in the ocean

Swimming over the side is an excellent way of keeping the body in top condition when at sea. The single-hander must take the greatest care that his boat does not sail away from him when he is overboard swimming – this is a more real danger than it might appear. The speed of a boat is deceptive to a man in the water and a sudden increase of wind, which may not be apparent at water level, can move a boat very rapidly away from a man in the sea. Sharks are an obvious danger but possibly one that is over-rated – the single-hander is usually aware of it when sharks are around his boat. If he does not venture too far and always leaves a long line overboard he should be able to swim in safety providing conditions are suitable. He should always use a snorkelling mask to keep a wary eye under the water. The refreshment and reinvigoration of a swim in the ocean is remarkable.

## Climbing on board

Apart from swimming for pleasure, a man by himself must be able to climb on board his boat from the water, either for'ard or aft, quickly and easily. Some boats are difficult to climb aboard, having high freeboard and few useful hand holds but

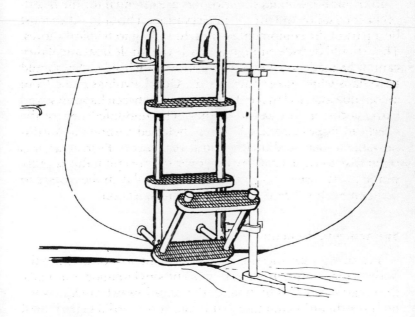

*If the steering vane is unsuitable for clambering on board, steps with below-water extension should be fitted.*

practice in harbour before the voyage starts usually finds a way. Regardless of a man's agility, climbing aboard may be slow and laborious until he is familiar with every hand and foothold. There may be many reasons for the single-hander to go overboard at sea – to clear weed or a rope from the propellor, to free the engine water intake or the lavatory from some blockage or to inspect an underwater fitting. Usually the steering vane can be used for climbing aboard but if this is not possible for any reason, a ladder should be permanently fixed to the stern with an extra two rungs which can be let down from the water so as to

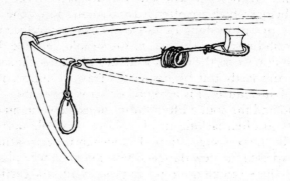

*Develop ideas for climbing back on board in the event of falling over. Here is one.*

give a foothold below water level. Climbing over the bow is not always easy if the boat has no bowsprit and bobstay. In this case a length or rope with a bight in it should be kept hanging overboard for'ard, close enough to the water for a swimmer to reach. It should be made fast and a bight secured on deck by a piece of thin twine which can be broken by a smart jerk from below, releasing a suitable length of rope. It takes practice to perfect the technique of climbing aboard. To the single-hander it is an essential drill.

## Good health at sea

Most of the maladies which afflict us on shore are caused fundamentally by the way in which we treat our bodies – what we give them to eat, to drink and how we use them physically. The ease and comparative luxury of modern living are the body's worst enemies and it reacts by visiting on us a variety of infirmities. In many cases our reaction to these diseases, either real or imagined, is to treat them with a huge and complex assortment of drugs designed to suppress the symptoms of our ailment while taking little account of what causes it in the first instance. The man alone at sea can break free of this depressing syndrome. His new life will satisfy many of the basic needs of human beings which are often frustrated on shore – the sense of freedom, the astonishing quality of well-being induced by the clean, fresh breezes of the ocean, the simple, sensible diet, the hard physical work, the need for mental alertness, the satisfying routine and lastly but by no means least in importance, the reality of adventure. It is adventure that is appealing – it gives the mind and the soul a lift, a flutter of excitement, an edge of keenness so often lacking in life ashore. A whole new vista is opened by the very suggestion of a lone voyage across the ocean – new experiences, new dangers, new delights, new places and people – there can be no mind so ground into the earth by the travail of life that cannot lift to such a vision.

## Ill health unlikely at sea

All these things together make, above all else, for a healthy man, free of the paltry and undignified afflictions of the shore. There is no reason in the world, given sensible care and attention to obvious precautions, for a man alone at sea to be ill. Even common accidents, once he is free of the psychological stresses of the shore, are unlikely to happen to him. He will, almost without doubt, end his voyage a fitter man in mind and body without recourse to drugs, medicines, potions and all the varied hotch potch of prophylactics that afflict life ashore. Having committed himself to the ocean a healthy man, let him with the same faith and trust allow the ocean to keep him healthy.

# 7 BAD WEATHER

Sooner or later the single-hander who sails the oceans of the world must meet extreme weather conditions – the survival storm. It is perhaps this inevitable confrontation with the supreme force of nature that drives him to chance his nerve and his knowledge against the power of the sea. It is not a challenge – only an arrogant fool will believe that he can challenge the omnipotence of the ocean – rather it is a supplication to be granted the strength and confidence that comes to a man who has passed through the physical and spiritual experience of a storm at sea. It will bring to the surface his authentic qualities and failings, revealing those qualities and failings to himself with the unanswerable clarity of truth. Every single-hander will rehearse over in his mind the action he will take when faced with a survival storm. He will have, somewhere in his consciousness, a picture, a mental conception of what the storm may hold for him and how he will face it. When it comes, the storm may be unlike his imaginings – each has its own individuality, its specific identity and no two are alike. It is the knowledge that by his own skill and nerve he can bring himself and his boat safely through storm conditions, that sets the single-hander apart and gives him the fulfilment that he set out to achieve when he first left his home shores.

## Wind behind

The single-hander's attitude to the storm will depend on the circumstances of each one. If his yacht is in the open ocean with the wind favourable in direction and the fetch to land infinite, the problem will resolve itself into a simple and uncomplicated endeavour to do the best for his ship and the best for himself, so that at no time does the storm get the upper hand. The barometer and the sky will have made the weather's intention perfectly clear. There will have been a slow, inexorable fall in pressure, perhaps over the space of two or three days, the wind will freshen and back, cloud will thicken and lower, the seas will steadily increase. There is a certain quality about a rising storm at sea which marks it as unmistakable – the single-hander will be well aware of what is in store for him.

## Preparation

He will shorten sail as the wind increases – the mainsail will be reefed and soon taken off altogether perhaps to be replaced by a storm trysail or perhaps by a headsail alone. If he is wise, in the early stages he will have a good meal and put himself by a hot drink in a thermos flask. Hot tea is good but hot soup or Bovril or Marmite in which crusts of bread or biscuit can be soaked, is better. Nuts, raisins and chocolate should be stowed to hand – they are easy to digest and remarkably nourishing. He will make sure that he is warm and that he has on good wet-gear. It is of prime importance to keep dry and warm. Before he goes out of the cabin, or even before he opens the cabin hatch in bad weather, he must be fully protected against the wet. Only the most pressing emergency – a crisis that will not wait – should persuade the single-hander to go on deck without his wet-gear.

Wet and cold are the absolute enemies of rational, sensible thought and action and should be avoided at all costs. Likewise the single-hander's bedding and the cabin settees should be kept dry. In a gale a yacht quickly becomes wet and uncomfortable inside unless care is taken. Apart from spray through an open hatch, every time the single-hander goes on deck he will bring wet into the cabin with him when he returns. In storm conditions humidity inside the cabin will be high and with no sun or through draught of dry air, everything soon becomes clammy and inhospitable. A solid fuel stove, if it can be kept alight, is worth its weight in gold.

He will do any routine jobs in good time such as filling navigation and cabin lamps and checking that all hatches are properly secured and covers properly fastened. The gear should be minutely checked for any weakness and lashings doubled where necessary, the DR should be run up. Careful preparations pay a high dividend in storm conditions.

Running before the wind is the only way to keep a yacht with her length and her ends in line with the run of the seas and it is in this position that she is safest. The problem is to keep her in line with the seas, or, as some yachts prefer, with the wind slightly on the quarter. As the wind freshens it may often change in direction, usually backing against the clock. In a short time the direction of the seas may become distorted, so that waves are encountered which are travelling at an angle of as much as twenty-five degrees to the general set. Waves in a gale travel at a speed of twenty-five knots so that a yacht is constantly overtaken by breaking seas. This situation demands a man on the helm who can swing the yacht's stern to meet the advancing waves. It is here that the single-hander is vulnerable and it is for this reason that careful preparation for storm conditions is indispensable.

If he is not already tired before the bad weather sets in and if he has prepared his supporting services properly so that he can eat, drink something hot and keep himself dry and comfortable without leaving the helm, he will be able to stay on deck and guide his boat through the seas for as long as the extreme conditions are likely to last. Every boat will vary in the amount of attention she needs in a storm. A heavy boat with a long straight keel may be the most sea kindly but this does not necessarily follow. Steadiness is the quality a boat requires in these conditions – the steadier she is, the easier will be the single-handers' lot. Good freeboard is a most valuable attribute, a stern which is high and full and a fine run aft under the water, so that the yacht does not leave a confused wake, are all qualities that the single-hander will appreciate in his boat.

## Surfing

As the wind increases so the seas become longer, the boat travels faster and becomes more difficult to manage. Most yachts will run before a gale without being manually steered either with some sail set for'ard or without, until she begins to surf on the wave tops. The moment this begins to happen she must be slowed down and she must be watched meticulously. A surfing yacht is quite unmanageable. She is, in fact, substantially lifted out of the water and borne along on a cushion of fast moving air and water mixed into an effervescent foam. She will not answer her helm and she will be capable of swinging round broadside to the seas. In this position she may be overwhelmed or turned over and she will be prey to heavy damage by the following wave breaking immediately on her when she is in a helpless position broadside to the seas. The power of a breaking wave to damage a yacht is astonishing. Heavy iron stanchions can be bent like childs' plasticine, stout wooden hatches can be broken, deck fittings can be torn adrift, solidly built and fastened houses can be wrenched from the deck.

## Adjusting the speed

The key to safety is to have the yacht travelling at the correct speed for the conditions and this speed will vary from boat to boat. It is a matter for the single-hander's judgement and common sense. If she is travelling too fast, the greatest danger and the easiest to fall into, she will surf. Not enough speed, on the other hand, makes her less manoeuvrable and liable to take heavy water on board or to be pitch-poled. This is normally only possible in very large seas which are seldom seen even by yachtsmen cruising the world, but it is more likely to happen in light yachts and those which are designed with a fine entry. Pitch-poling occurs when a boat buries her bow while her stern is lifted and swept forward by the following wave so that she falls head over heels. More often, when this happens, the yacht turns through a right angle and suffers no worse fate than a severe knock-down – if she does go right over she is likely to break her mast.

The classic method of slowing a boat down is to stream warps and its effectiveness is indisputable. Heavy, fibre rope is best for the job although any warp is effective. It should be dragged astern in a bight, one end fastened to each quarter. Care should be taken to take the turns out of the rope as it goes over so that it does not twist up. The effect is remarkable – a narrow path will form immediately astern where the seas only occasionally break and surfing will cease although the odd crest may still break aboard. It is possible, even easy to go too slowly when running with streamed warps so that the yacht loses her liveliness and cannot be steered. In this case she may ship heavy seas over her

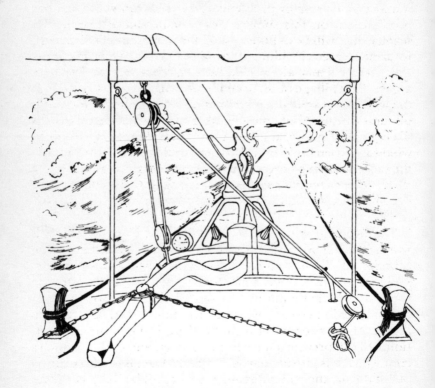

*Heavy fibre rope, dragged astern in a bight, quells surfing and breaking waves in storm conditions.*

quarters and these may be destructive. Sometimes she will steady and become tractable if a small headsail is set in these conditions.

## Oil

If the wind continues to rise and the sea to increase in size so that the yacht ships heavy, dangerous water it may be necessary to use oil – a time-honoured method of weathering extreme conditions. There are several ways of doing this, none of them pleasant or easy – oil is messy stuff and unless it is carefully used it may create as many problems as it solves. Much of what has been written on this subject, not least in official manuals of seamanship, will be of little value to the single-hander. Oil bags, for instance, require filling from a can or drum – a near impossible task for a man alone in the heaving cabin of a small yacht in a gale. The spillage of oil would be as dangerous to his safety as the waves. It is sometimes recommended that the engine sump oil should be used but unless nothing else is available, this too, is likely to be a messy, unpleasant business. Spreading of oil to windward when hove-to is also a practical impossibility because the yacht is making headway and will immediately sail out of the slick. When running before a following sea in extreme conditions, however, oil can be of great practical value if used correctly.

The problem is to release it in very small quantitites. It is worth carrying on board a few tins, not larger than a half-gallon capacity, of raw linseed oil which is the best for this purpose. When required, a single small hole should be made in the tin with a spike, the tin put into an old kit bag or a strong pillow-case or cushion cover. The whole lot should then be streamed astern. About twenty feet from the stern is the optimum position. Oil will prevent a wave from forming, but it will not quell a crest which has already started to break. The oil will leak slowly out of the tin and will impregnate the bag and diffuse itself over the sea immediately in the yacht's wake. This method allows the single-hander to use oil without getting his boat and his gear in a slippery, sticky and smelly mess. A half-gallon tin will give him as much as an hour's respite from steering in a following storm. He can use the time to rest, to feed himself and to rehabilitate himself for the next part of his battle.

## Use of drugs

With his boat tight above and below decks, his gear sound and he himself, fed, warm and reasonably dry a storm becomes a battle of endurance. If he hangs on for long enough and is able to keep his boat from damage, the single-hander knows that he must come through. A well-found yacht of sensible design and properly handled can survive any storm in the open ocean. It is the land that destroys boats, not the sea. In harbours, yachts are torn from their moorings in destructive storms and hurled adrift along with roofs, chimney-pots, trees, motor cars and anything movable. Clear of the land, a well-found yacht will be taken to leeward with the storm and left to make her way back when better times break through. There may be hurricanes with winds of such ferocity that nothing can stand against them – in these circumstances a good yacht will have as much chance of coming through as anything. The problem for the single-hander is to keep himself in a fit state to think clearly, to make sensible decisions and to preserve for himself the physical strength to carry them out. When he gets tired he will have great difficulty in maintaining concentration and he may find that even the will to survive is weakened. The noise of the storm and the aspect of destructive violence may sap his will to fight on. He will be an easy prey to pressimism – the conviction that all is lost and that nothing he can do will match the power of the storm.

In these moments drugs such as Benzedrine are of doubtful value. They give temporary alertness to a tired brain and they may for a time prolong a tired man's ability to concentrate, but when the effect wears off they leave him in a worse state. This may be acceptable in an emergency in a crewed yacht but for a single-hander it is potentially disastrous. A slug of brandy is a good temporary stimulant – it gives a flush of warmth and comfort which reaches through to every part of the body – but its effect soon passes and, in the long run, it probably does more harm than good. Concentrated glucose in the form of Dextrosol tablets is probably better than anything. The glucose is absorbed directly into the blood stream and gives the body immediate energy. It also relieves mental tension and allows the brain to work coolly at times of nervous strain. It is a natural substance and does not seem to have any reactive after effects – neither is it harmful or habit forming.

## The sea anchor

When the gale is in a contrary direction the single-hander will be unwilling to turn and run before it because of the distance lost. He will keep on under reduced sail until the strain on his boat and the wear and tear on his own nerves becomes intolerable and then he will heave-to. Most cruising yachts will heave-to and lie in reasonable comfort through foul weather unless the conditions become so bad that even the smallest sail is too much. For the single hander, lying hove-to is the easiest way of weathering a storm because the yacht will look after herself, requiring no hand on the helm. She will give to the seas, making some leeway, with a small headsail hauled a'weather and a storm trysail or heavily reefed mainsail sheeted hard in. This rig should hold her steady so that she makes minimal headway and rides easily over the seas. Ketches and yawls have an advantage over single-masted yachts in that they can be kept close to the wind and the seas without the mainsail being set.

If possible the yacht should be kept moving slowly ahead as in this way she will lie more naturally and will not suffer undue strain on the rudder. The use of a sea anchor when hove-to depends to a great extent on the yacht. Although a sea anchor may hold her nicely into the seas with very little or no sail set, she is more likely to lie beam to the seas and she may even develop stern-way thus imposing strains on the rudder which may well lead to a breakage. The sea anchor is of little use over the bow but may be invaluable over the stern. In normal circumstances there should be little strain on a yacht hove-to and little for the single-hander to worry about unless she begins to be struck by heavy seas.

## Lying a-try

The crash of a big sea hitting the top sides of a yacht, the thunder of heavy water on the coach roof and the shake and judder as the yacht reels to the enormous strains of this type of punishment, will soon convince the single-hander that he can no longer safely remain hove-to. Sooner or later the sheer weight and strength of the sea will begin to damage his boat. If he has sea room he may turn and run before it, counting the loss of miles as a small price to pay for safety, or he may lie a-try, allowing the yacht to fend for herself with no sail set. Many yachts lie very sweetly a-try although it is not usually a comfortable position as they tend to heel considerably to the wind and to be thrown about by the seas. They also may be vulnerable to a knock-down in very strong winds and heavy seas. It may be necessary to reduce windage by stripping the mast of surplus gear. A gaff cutter may have as many as seven halyards aloft which together offer considerable top hamper. Most yachts lie a-try with the wind a little abaft the beam and often they give so readily to the seas that very little water comes aboard. It may be feasible to use oil in these circumstances because the yacht has virtually no way on. In this case the oil tin should be hung over the weather side amidships, or it may be effective to pump oil out through the yacht's lavatory discharge. By lying a-try instead of running from a gale the single-hander may save 100 miles of distance in a long lived contrary blow.

## Clawing off a lee shore

The real test of seamanship and endurance for the single-hander will occur if he is caught in a severe on-shore gale when he is close to an inhospitable coast with no safe refuge under his lee. The best defence against this danger is not to allow it to arise. There are many such dangerous coastlines in all parts of the world. The west European coastline from Cape St. Vincent in the south of Portugal to the English Channel and beyond, is riddled with them. The only really safe course is to make an offing while the weather is fair of such magnitude as to give him an ample margin of safety to leeward. The pilot books will tell him what likelihood there is of meeting dangerous weather – he should take good heed of them and then allow an extra margin for his own peace of mind. If he should find himself with dangerous water to leeward in a rising gale, all his efforts must be directed towards keeping his boat to windward. Unless the wind is blowing directly onto the shore, he should select the tack which will allow him to point most off shore. He should remember that he will probably make less leeway in a rough sea by sailing with the wind slightly free than by pinching her too close. He should be certain never to miss stays if he is forced to come about as this will lose him priceless yards to leeward – if necessary he should use the engine to help his boat round. It is a prodigious task to keep a small boat from being swept to leeward in a storm – the force of the wind and the seas is so over-powering that it takes a good boat, well handled, to hold her position. By careful steering and concentration the single-hander may be able to sail his boat across wind without losing distance to leeward but she will run the risk of damage either by

SEA ANCHOR BELOW
SURFACE

*Sea anchor: primarily of use to reduce drift when running off becomes essential and dangers lie to leeward.*

being overwhelmed by wind and sea or by breakage. In the last resort, to keep afloat, he may have to run even towards a danger. In this case he should strip all windage aloft, stream warps and a sea anchor and drop his bower anchor over the stern with all the chain he has in the locker. This might reduce his leeward drift to as little as one knot which should give him a few hours of grace to allow for an improvement in the weather. A sea anchor, to be of any real use, must be very strongly made.

What is sometimes called luck plays its part in weathering a severe storm – a shift of wind in the right direction, a sail which blows out and eases the yacht in a severe squall, the choice of a course which takes her clear of danger. More often it is the single-hander's care for himself and his gear and his ability to turn a difficult situation to his own advantage that brings the boat through. The sea is no respecter of persons – whether a man alone, who has trusted himself to the gale, survives or perishes is of no consequence to the relentless and inevitable passage of the storm. A man who does not underestimate the sea's power and who has learnt to give it his full respect, is more likely to survive because his actions will be governed and guided by a proper understanding.

# 8 CLOSE WORK AND ANCHORING

Proper forethought and a few simple aids can help the single-hander to carry out tight harbour moves with a neat, effortless efficiency which are often bungled in crewed yachts. Coming up to a mooring or anchoring in a crowded harbour, under the eyes of a multiude, or twisting and turning into a tight yacht marina berth can tax even an accomplished crew. The man alone must make his dispositions in advance and provide himself with all he needs readily to hand. He will have no time to be rummaging for fenders or ropes in a locker while his boat is being carried through an anchorage by a brisk flood tide, with yachts on all sides glistening with bright and expensive paintwork. If he makes a mistake, he may find the situation out of his control in a bewilderingly short time. Boats have a habit of getting the bit between their teeth and running amok if they are once allowed to get the upper hand. Once out of his tight control, a boat in a strong wind and a tideway may be too heavy and recalcitrant for a man alone to manage. Damage can accrue with frightening rapidity. In these circumstances the single-hander will get scant sympathy. So far from being excused he will be the more harshly blamed and will be accused of irresponsibility for endangering other people's property. For this reason he must be quite certain that he can at all times handle his boat by himself with no risk to himself or others.

## Picking up a mooring

With practice, coming up to a mooring is often easier under sail. Under sail the operation will be given proper thought and will be planned in such a way that the boat comes naturally to rest in the required spot. Under engine a boat is often brought to a mooring or an anchorage athwart tide or wind, with little regard to how she will behave when the engine is stopped. The single-hander will leave the helm and run for'ard to grasp a mooring which has been hidden from him by the yacht's bow for a minute or more, to find it tantalizingly beyond his reach and the yacht driving down wind or tide towards some danger.

He should never attempt to pick up a mooring over the bow, a difficult operation for a man alone either under engine or sail. Rather he should prepare a length of nylon warp with a spring clip spliced into one end. This should be rove from the bitts for'ard, through the fairlead, outside everything and aft in way

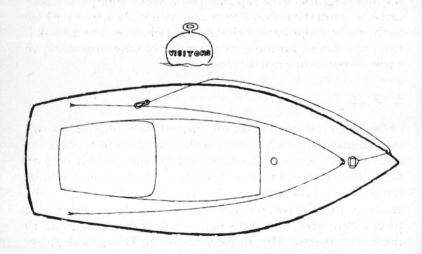

*Never attempt to pick up a mooring over the bow. Single-hander needs prearranged line for use amidships.*

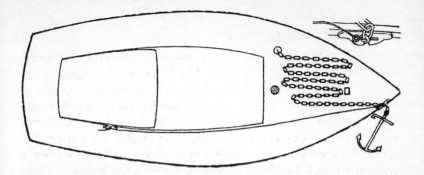

*Chain flaked on deck with anchor release line led to cockpit.*

of the cockpit where the clip can be hooked over a cleat or attached to a runner or the yacht's rail or lifeline. She can then be brought up with the mooring alongside amidships so that the single-hander can lean over where the freeboard is least, grasp the mooring, attach the clip and let the whole thing go. Then he can take down the sails at leisure and haul in slack over the bow as the yacht drops back with the tide. If he uses a boathook it should be short, no more than three feet long, so that it can easily be put to one side after use.

## Anchoring

Coming up to an anchor, the single-hander should have his gear prepared in such a way that he has no need to leave the helm to drop anchor. The chain or rope should be hauled on deck and flaked so that it will run free. The anchor should be hung over the bow and secured with a tripping line which can be released from the cockpit. This can be done quite easily with a piece of brass rod passed through a link of the chain, to which the line is attached. He can then pick his anchorage with an eye to the tide, the wind, the offing, the echo sounder and the position of other boats. When he is in the optimum position he can let go by a sharp jerk on the tripping line and then attend to sail stowing while the chain runs out to its stop.

103

## Engine ready

When picking up a mooring or coming up to an anchorage under sail it is always as well to have the engine ready for immediate use – it is essential to have an engine which can be brought into use at a moment's notice. Sailing up to a mooring is most useful and satisfying and should be practised wherever possible. It makes the single-hander aware of his boat's behaviour in all manner of different conditions of wind and tide and it ensures that when for one reason or another it is really necessary for him to carry out some difficult manoeuvre under sail, he knows how to do it.

At the same time, at least for the sake of other boats in the anchorage, the engine should be available at the touch of a button. Reliable electric starting for an engine is a great comfort to a man by himself. If the engine is a diesel in good condition it should start without hesitation – the fuel should always be turned on, the engine left in ahead gear and the throttle set at a position to give slow revs. In case of a misjudgement under sail it can be used to give the extra power needed to convert a failure into a well carried out exercise.

It is no part of good seamanship to have on board a boat an engine which cannot be used when it is needed because it is not in a state of readiness or proper order. The engine is just as much a part of the motive power of a modern yacht as are the sails and should be as efficient. This is not to say that it should be wholly relied on at any time, but if it is to be carried on board, it must be at all times in top condition. An engine in a boat which is not in this condition is so much wasted space and effort – it should either be put right or got rid of.

The engine uses prime space, it slows the boat with propellor drag, it is oily, smelly and a source of insupportable frustration. Equally a good and reliable engine is an abiding pleasure and a comfort to a man alone. He will delight in its smooth, quiet running and will love it for its willingness to spring to his aid when he needs it. A petrol engine may take longer to start because the fuel may have to be turned on and the carburettor flooded. This should be done before entering or leaving harbour under sail in case it should suddenly be required.

## Ground tackle

The anchor is probably the heaviest and most awkward piece of equipment on board a yacht and effectively it sets a limit on the size of boat for general cruising that can be handled by a man alone. Ground tackle must be heavy enough to hold in a strong blow but it must be light enough for the chain and the anchor to be manhandled aboard in difficult conditions. It is equally poor seamanship to be provided with ground tackle which is too light or to have an anchor and cable which are too heavy for practical use. The single-hander must compromise between these extremes. For all purpose cruising he should carry a CQR, or possibly a Danforth and a Fisherman type anchor. Both the CQR and the Danforth have excellent holding power in mud or sand or any reasonably soft bottom which the plough or flukes

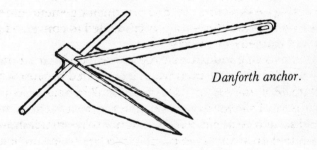

*Danforth anchor.*

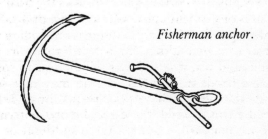

*Fisherman anchor.*

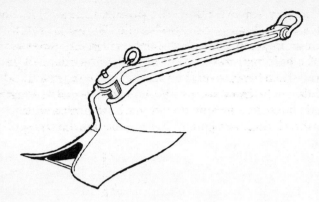

*CQR or "plow" anchor*

can penetrate. On a hard bottom or a bottom with a cover of weed or kelp these anchors are useless and the ordinary Fisherman must be used. The smallest string of weed round the plough of a CQR will prevent it from holding. On the other hand, having tremendous holding power for their size, provided the bottom is suitable, patent anchors must find favour with the single-hander. In a strange harbour he will be tempted to use his CQR because of its lightness, but he should make quite sure the boat is properly brought up before he goes to sleep.

It is also important for a man alone to have the chain fastened to the anchor by a shackle which can be undone quickly – an ordinary galvanized shackle will rust up and require time and effort to get clear if he needs to change the anchor quickly. A stainless shackle may be best, provided it is properly moused with stainless wire, or a senhouse slip, again provided it is properly moused. The Fisherman anchor, although it is heavy and difficult to handle for man by himself, has the virtue of reliability.

## Anchor weight

There is a simple method of doubling the holding power of an anchor, which must be of the greatest interest to the man alone because it may solve for him the problem of using a heavy enough anchor which he can also handle. The use of a "Chum" weight or an improvised anchor weight will give approximately double the holding power. "Chum" is a saddle made of galvanized iron which hangs over the anchor chain or rope and can be lowered down the chain to any desired depth. It can be weighted with lead "biscuits" to suit the strength of wind and tide. By holding the chain in a bight, "Chum" ensures that the pull on

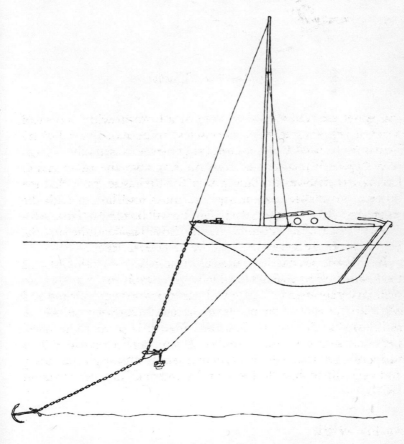

*Weight, such as "Chum", on anchor cable will double holding power.*

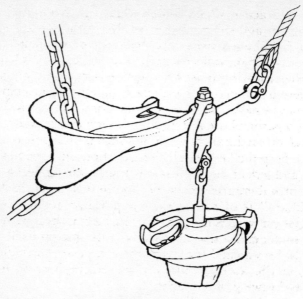

*"Chum" anchor weight*

the anchor is always horizontally along the bottom. The anchor can never be jerked upwards and broken out of the ground however rough the conditions. If "Chum's" line is made fast at the shrouds the yacht lies to a bridle which keeps the chain clear of the bow and seems to hold her steady even if a strong wind is forcing her across the tide. If it should be necessary to anchor in an exposed place, or if a strong wind sets in after the yacht has brought up, "Chum" can make the difference between un-easiness and the comfortable security of heavy and reliable ground tackle. A "Chum" weight can easily be improvised from a large bow shackle and any convenient weight, preferably of lead.

## Rope or chain

The single-hander, particularly if he has a light, displacement boat, will be tempted to use nylon for his anchor warp in place of chain, a practice which finds increasing favour as boats become lighter and chain more expensive. Although attractive because of its lightness, nylon is probably less convenient for the single-hander. Chain will stow itself in the locker as it is hauled aboard whereas nylon must be coiled on deck and then taken below where it will occupy more space than the same length of chain. It may be easier to coil a nylon anchor warp onto a drum, in the way a garden hose is stowed. Although it is usual to use a length of chain on the anchor itself to which the warp is attached in order to keep the line of pull along the bottom, a nylon warp will snub and jerk at the yacht's bow. It may foul against a rock or other protuberance on the bottom and damage itself by chafe. "Chum" is of even greater importance to the single-hander if nylon warp is used – it will ensure that the light nylon does not snub against the yacht's bow or the anchor itself. The line should be watched for chafe where it passes through the "Chum" saddle as there may be movement here with the pitching and yawing of the yacht.

Many yachts have a windlass on the foredeck for heaving the anchor, the chain falling through a hawse hole in the deck into a locker where it will usually look after itself, not requiring special stowage. A single-hander will find a windlass of great use in breaking out an anchor which is firmly embedded in mud or sand but once the anchor is free, he will want to heave in the chain hand over hand so as to get it in quickly. The windlass should be designed in such a way that this can be done. With some designs of windlass it is not easy to get the chain free of the gipsy to haul it by hand and this may waste the single-hander valuable minutes when he needs to be attending to the ship. If the windlass is right for'ard, where the deck is narrow, it is not always easy to handle the anchor by hand and the operation of hauling in chain and getting the anchor aboard is cramped, difficult and slow.

## Mast winch

A windlass or winch attached to the mast is often the best answer for a man by himself. The chain will lead through the

109

deck and via a wooden trunk or a pipe to the locker immediately for'ard of the mast, where there is ample room for it to stow itself and where its weight is probably best disposed. Standing on the broad part of the deck it is easier to get a good purchase on the chain which will run over the gipsy as it is hauled and be pulled down into the locker by its own weight. At the same time the single-hander can look around him and see where his boat is being carried. A mast windlass usually has a crank if extra power is needed to break the anchor free, but care must be taken that it is securely bolted to the mast and further fastened right round the mast with large stainless Jubilee clips. These windlasses should not be used where the mast does not pass through the deck to the keelson.

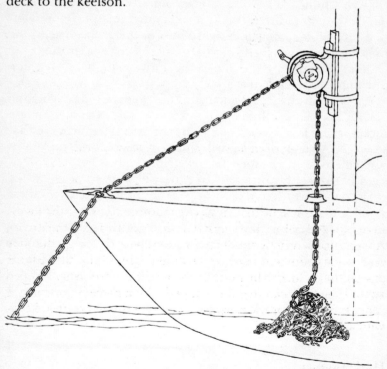

*Anchor winch on mast may be a better answer than a foredeck site.*

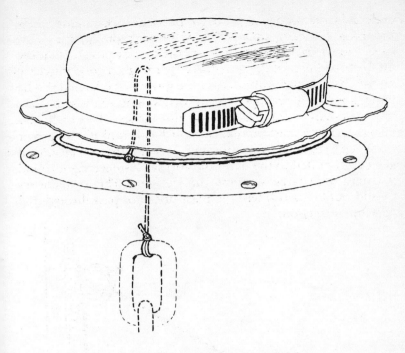

*Anchor chain hawse pipe waterproofed for sea.*

The chain must be unshackled from the anchor and the hawse hole blocked before the single-hander ventures into the ocean. A length of synthetic small stuff should be attached to the bare end of the chain and made fast round the lip of the hawse hole, so that the chain can be pulled up out of the locker when needed again. The hole can then be stopped with a piece of motor tyre inner tube kept for the purpose, which is fastened round the lip with a Jubilee clip.

## Cable stopper

A cable stopper is invaluable for a man by himself. A senhouse slip attached to a short length of wire or chain from

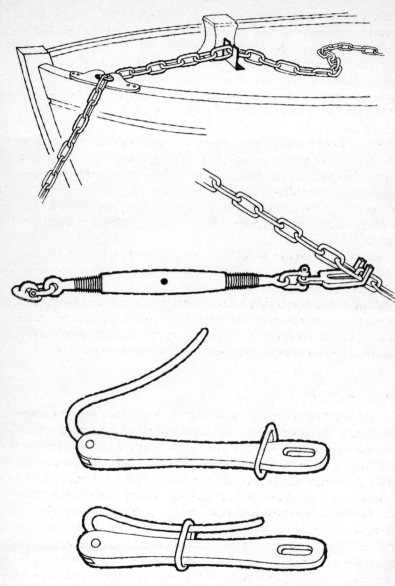

*Senhouse slip, devil's claw and deck bracket: all systems for holding an anchor chain.*

an eyebolt through the deck or some solid base, serves well. Unlike a "Devil's Claw" type of stopper, it can be let go when there is strain on the chain. An alternative is to have an iron right-angle bracket fastened to the deck in way of the chain's lead, slotted to take the link so that the chain can simply be dropped into it. A cable stopper enables a man by himself to leave the foredeck at a second's notice without losing his hard won chain.

The inboard end of the anchor chain should be fastened in the locker not with a shackle – it may be difficult to undo in a rush – but with turns of small stuff which can be cut free with a knife or, better still a short length of synthetic line fastened with a slip knot. One day it may be necessary to slip the cable and in such an emergency the man alone is unlikely to have leisure to spare.

The single-hander would do well to mark his chain clearly, red, white and blue at 5, 10 and 15 fathoms is easy to remember. The full number of links should be painted with each colour, making confusion difficult. Anchor bearings must be taken as a matter of course as soon as the yacht is brought up, either with a hand bearing compass or by lining up two fixed objects on the shore. The bearings or marks should be noted in the log.

## Harbour work

Coming in to a strange yacht marina, especially at night when there may be no one to help him moor and when the whole community of yachtsmen is asleep, the single-hander must have everything prepared in advance. If the weather is boisterous outside it may not be possible to have ropes and fenders and boat hook on deck and in position – in this case he should either lie quietly within the marina and make ready, or pick up a buoy, if there is one, or tie up bows to another boat while he spies out the land and selects his berth. He will be unpopular if he blunders about in the marina making a noise like thunder as he thumps on to the pontoons, or if he·revs his engine and causes a disturbance by crashing alongside other boats. He should have ropes and fenders ready on both sides as it is often impossible to know which side to the yacht will lie and he should turn his engine off as soon as he is able so that his close neighbours can heave a sigh of relief, turn on their sides and resume snoring.

## Anchor work

Bringing home the anchor in a strong blow may be the most difficult task in the single-hander's calendar and he should take the greatest care that his boat does not run out of control and that he does not quickly exhaust his strength. Here again, with a little practice it is often easier to recover an anchor under sail than with the engine but in either case the chain should be persuaded into the boat not by brute strength so much as by guile. Under reduced sail a yacht will easily tack up to her anchor, the chain itself helping her through stays on each tack. As she comes athwart the scope on each tack chain can be recovered when it is slack and held by the chain stopper when the strain comes on it. When she is shortened up she should sail the anchor out of the ground by herself.

Under engine, with no other person to steer, it will be difficult to keep the yacht head to the wind and sea and the single-hander will find himself running back and forth between the tiller, the engine control and the foredeck. It may also be difficult to break the anchor out of the ground under engine. If the tide is rising it is better to belay the chain and let nature do the heavy work. To be avoided at all costs is an attempt to heave in chain against the pull of a strong wind and tide – there is no activity on board more exhausting. In good conditions a windlass is useful but more often than not, the chain will have to be manhandled aboard for the sake of speed. If the yacht is dragging towards a dangerous lee shore the single-hander may decide that the only way to save his boat is to slip the cable.

## Amenities

Some method of jib furling gear, or roller gear for a headsail is of great value in coming up to a mooring. The Wykeham-Martin type gear is good but the standard ball bearing should be replaced by a roller bearing in a greased cage, which can easily be changed for a spare in case of stiffness or seizure. These cage bearings are easy to get, in most sizes, but not so easily in stainless steel. The modern staysail furling and reefing gears may be efficient, providing that they work consistently, but this is not equipment likely to appeal to the single-handed cruising man who should always opt for simplicity and reliability.

Another essential is a simple method of fixing the helm in a given position when it is necessary to leave it unattended for a few minutes to run to the foredeck, tend a sail or fetch something from below. The easiest method is by a small link chain which lies across the top of the tiller and can be slipped into a metal claw which is fastened to the top of the tiller. This chain can be shackled to the coaming or the deck on one side of the ship and fastened with a lashing on the other side so that its tension can be adjusted. In some wind-operated steering gears the chain is standard. The top of the tiller in way of the claw must be protected from chafe by a strip of copper nailed across it.

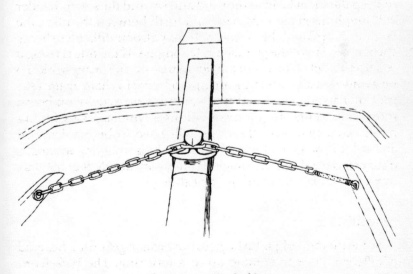

*Chain type tiller lashing.*

Another amenity for the single-hander is provision for the trim lines of his steering vane to be carried for'ard to the cabin hatch so that the yacht can be trimmed on course without the single-hander coming on deck when no sail adjustment is needed. Some single-handed yachts have the falls of the halyards led to the cockpit so that sail can be taken off without stirring for'ard. This would seem to add more complications to life than it saves, cluttering the cockpit with coils of rope and requiring extra blocks and leads. A better method of stowing the coils of the halyards when the sails are hoisted is to have a wooden cleat for each halyard screwed to the mast so that the coils can be hung up off the deck and out of the way. A piece of light line permanently attached to each cleat can be used to lash the coils in place. In this way the falls of the halyards are kept separate one from another and can be got ready for lowering quickly

A small grapnel with a length of line attached is a handy implement to have on the cabin top with the assorted bits and pieces of gear that usually find a home there on a cruising yacht.

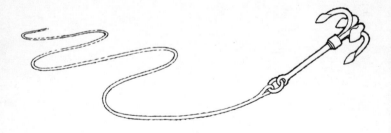

*Work out your own handy implements. Here is a simple grapnel — if not always appreciated by some harbour authorities!*

It can be thrown up on to a quay and used to haul the yacht alongside, or cast over a buoy beyond the reach of the boat hook, or dropped overboard as a marker with a float or fender attached or used to drag the bottom for a lost anchor chain or to catch the end of a rope round the propeller or to pick up a drifting dinghy or for all manner of vital uses. This small amenity will soon become a firm friend.

Each single-hander will have his own quirks and notions of what he needs to make life easier and to help him to do the work of at least two men, which at all times he must be able to do. Each will develop his own stratagems and his own short cuts and dodges so that he can find his way equally across the oceans of the world and in and out of the harbours, rivers, yacht marinas, shady lagoons and secret creeks of wherever he chooses for his cruising ground. He may appear eccentric but his eccentricities are born of the necessity to improvise so that his two eyes, two hands and one pair of legs can be in several different parts of his boat, performing several different tasks at one and the same time. The art of the thing is to make it all look easy.

# 9 TRADES AND TWINS

There may be single-handed voyagers fortunate enough, or perhaps provident enough, to be able to chose the exact type, size, rig and shape of boat they want for their venture. Most are less well provided, or well heeled and are content to make do with the boat they already have or the boat they can afford or the boat that happens to come their way. The art of sailing alone across the oceans is one which demands inventiveness, imagination and above all, the ability to improvise. These virtues, which are found to some extent in all lone voyagers, may be responsible for the astonishing variety of craft which can be seen under the command of a lone sailor. The most casual glance at any book describing lone voyages will reveal this phenomenon. Between Voss's Indian dug-out canoe *Tilikum* and the twelve foot *Sea Egg* in which John Riding sailed across the Pacific and the Atlantic oceans before he was drowned, lie an infinite variety of boats – large, small, fast, slow, comfortable and safe, wretched and hazardous. Very few boats are designed specifically to be sailed alone, except perhaps some of those for stunts or gambits such as single-handed races or some unusual undertaking. Those ordinary sailors who wish to indulge in this curious pastime must make their own adaptations and innovations.

Because of the relationship which grows up between a man alone and his boat after countless miles of ocean together, each single-hander will magnify the virtues and belittle the vices of his own vessel. Single-handed cruising is not competitive – each voyage is unique to itself and therefore there is no overall criterion or standard by which the boats can be judged. They all have their vices and their virtues – some tend towards one end of the compromise and some towards the other. It is this diversity which is found among the boats and among those that sail them, which lends to the activity much of its charm.

Long voyages under sail usually follow well-defined routes dictated by the prevailing winds. Nature has been prolific in this as in all her arrangements and by using the trade winds wisely and with patience a man can find his way under sail to almost every corner of the world with a free wind. For this reason the great sailing ships of the eighteenth and nineteenth centuries and for aeons before, were designed to sail down wind – they were poor performers to windward. The fore-and-aft rig was developed in coastal waters among local traders and fishermen where an urgent necessity existed to be able to sail close hauled – to claw off a lee shore, to land a catch up tide and up wind or to gain a harbour against a rising storm.

The sudden eclipse of the sailing ship after its gradual development over the whole of recorded time, when it had reached a zenith of human endeavour, technically and artistically and in terms of human effort, resulted in an abrupt stop to the development of square rig. Instead, the new age of technology switched its efforts to the fore-and-aft Bermudian rig on which it lavished all the sophisticated expertise made possible by new skills and new materials such as stainless steel, high tensile wire, plastics and synthetic fibres. But for the man sailing by himself a highly developed windward sailing machine is both irrelevant and impractical – the first because most of his sailing time, as in the old days, will be down wind and the second because the huge areas of headsail which are standard to a modern yacht cannot properly be handled by a man alone. The single-hander may do better to cast his thinking back towards the middle of the compromise when choosing, or more likely adapting, his rig.

## Down-wind sails

Fore-and-aft rig is an inferior instrument for sailing down the trades – particularly the high aspect ratio Bermudian mainsail is inefficient in a following wind. However, the single-hander will have to make the best of it for there is no alternative to the fore-and-aft rig. Square yards in small yachts, although they have their attractions and their devotees, are not practical, least of all for a man by himself. Square sails are clumsy to set, clumsy to stow and the extra weight aloft reduces stability and makes for heavy rolling. A yard may also put unacceptable twist strains on the mast of a small yacht. Twin staysails offer the standard solution to the problem of how to sail a small boat through the trade winds for days and weeks on end. If properly thought out and rigged they are easy to handle and can be kept up for long periods without fear of damage or chafe.

Twin staysails should be as large as can reasonably be accommodated and handled by a man alone. The trade winds can vary in strength, even in the course of a single day, between force seven or even force eight on the Beaufort scale and a light

*When sailing down wind, traditional fore-and-aft sails should be handed and twin running sails set.*

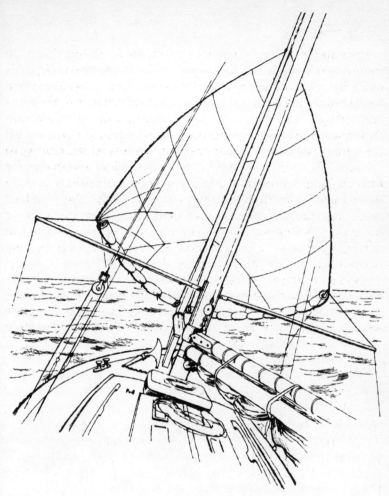

*Twin headsails must be capable of being reefed.*

breeze, therefore the twins must be large and capable of being reefed. If they are big sails at least two rows of reef points should be provided. Rows of eyelets through which a continuous line is rove are difficult to work with on a rolling foredeck and traditional reef points should be used. Unless the yacht is equipped with twin fore stays, the sails should each run on its

121

own, collapsing stay. The bottom end of these small wire stays should have a rope tail which passes through a block, one each side of the stem head or, perhaps, the bowsprit and is led to a cleat in way of the mast. The single-hander can then stand at the mast, hank the sail to the slack stay, attach the halyard and then haul it out to the stem without ever going for'ard himself. When the twins are not being used these stays can hang in the shrouds out of the way, secured by a piece of shock cord. The sails should be of light material; six ounce Terylene (Dacron) is strong enough and is easy to handle. It is a good plan to have the twins in a different colour from the working sails so that they can easily be identified in the locker.

## Twin booms

Booms should be of wood rather than alloy – they can more easily be repaired – and they should set independently of the sails themselves. In this way the single-hander can prepare the sails and the booms separately as two distinct tasks so that he is not left with two or more operations to carry out at the same time when the sails are hoisted. The booms should attach to the mast by ringed slides running in a short track one on each side of the mast so that the inboard pressure is directly against the solid mast. The inboard ends of the booms are fitted with spring fastenings which attach to the slides. Jaws which fit against the mast are unsatisfactory. They do not stay in position and however well they are served they will chafe the mast. The booms should be supported before the sail is set by short strops from the shrouds or, better still, from the side-light screens, which fasten round them with a loop and toggle or a slip knot. These can be let go once the twin is hoisted and the weight taken by the sail. Before the sail goes up the guy to the stern should be rigged and set up to a mark at the cleat which will give the right tension when the sail is set. Lastly a swivel block at the end of the boom carries the sheet which can be fastened to the sail with a spring clip and cleated on the inboard end of the boom. The sail is then hoisted, run out to the end of the boom, the strop released and the guy trimmed.

Twins should not be too high for their width – the top of a sail will do little work and a better and fuller spread may be achieved if the sail is lower. The luff ropes should be of small size rope, not wire and the foot should be cut with a good roach to give extra area. The tack of the sails should be set as far for'ard as it can be – half way along a bowsprit if one is carried – so as to give the sails the maximum lift and a good air flow.

## Twins and square rig

Running down the trades under twin staysails is one of the greatest joys in the single-hander's experience. The yacht will reach her optimum cruising speed very easily under this rig and with no strain or worry – she seems to lift and fly forward as if inspired by the genius of the trade itself. The sensation must be akin to the ecstasy of sailing under square rig. A man can marvel and be humbled in the same way at the harmonious blending of overwhelming strength with the fragile piecing together of materials, which is a small yacht. The yacht under twins and the square-rigger are at opposite ends of the scale, but it is the same scale, governed by the same laws and principles. In both the wit and ingenuity of man combines with nature – draws its strength from nature without plundering or perverting or despoiling her.

With twins set and the trade piping, the deck is clear, the mainsail is furled and at rest on the boom gallows, the helm is easy with no more than a touch either way to keep the yacht on course, the motion is rhythmic and restful and the sea flies by without fuss, the log spins off the knots. The sails themselves are pregnant with wind their gentle, sensuous curves all urging the yacht forward. The strain on halyards, blocks, booms, guys, sheets and the sails themselves is all a steady even strain tending to draw the yacht upwards and on rather than to force her through the seas. It is all a delight which has to be experienced to be understood. The single-hander can with justice, stand in his cockpit, look around him and marvel at the experience he is creating for himself.

123

## Mainsail down-wind

The mainsail in most yachts is the biggest and heaviest sail on board and is the single-hander's work horse which he depends on to drive his ship in all manner of circumstances. The twins are specialist sails suited only to their own conditions – he can manage without them if need be, as indeed he can live without any other sail on board except his main. Handling this large area of sail is fundamental to the running of the ship and he must be the master of it. He must be able to set it, lower it, reef it, furl it, and stow it in all conditions of wind and sea. It is imperative that he should be able to carry out any or all these operations to his mainsail on all points of sailing and regardless of the strength of the wind. Running before a strong and freshening wind the single-hander may be asleep. He may wake to find the yacht over pressed and a heavy sea running – it is surprising how quickly these conditions can spring up.

Often it is not immediately appreciated how rapidly the weather is changing until the yacht is suddenly found to be labouring under a full mainsail when she should be snugly reefed. The main boom, fully extended, may be lifting dangerously if it is a light spar or it may be dipping the wave crests as the yacht rolls and jerking at the sheet. The yacht will suddenly be found to be carrying far too much weather helm and the self-steering gear will be in danger of being overpowered. The wind may be so strong and the seas so heavy by now that it is dangerous to round up in order to drop the main. Running before it the wind is decreased by the yacht's own speed and the sail is full and therefore still. Once the helm is put down the yacht will feel the full force of the wind, her beam will be exposed to the breaking crests, she will surge ahead into the seas so that heavy water sweeps aboard, the apparent wind will be increased rather than decreased by her own speed and the mainsail will flap and shake so violently as to threaten the stays, the sail itself or even the mast. It is good seamanship and prudent custom when reefing or taking in sail on a run in a heavy sea and a rising wind to do so with the sail full of wind and not to round up.

## Mainsail downhaul

The Bermudian rig is vulnerable in these conditions. The yacht may have several sets of spreaders or cross trees and even with the main sheet hard in, the mainsail will be pressed against these. All the track slides will be pressed over to one side and the luff of the sail may be jammed solid. When the halyard is let go the sail will not fall down, indeed however the single-hander pulls and tugs at the luff he will not be able to move it. This is a

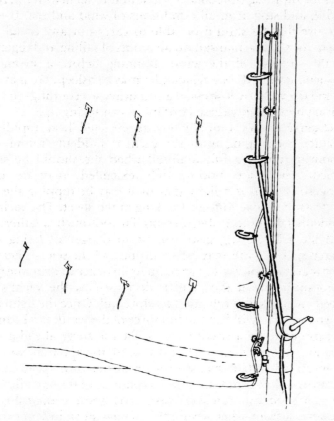

*Mainsail downhaul may be needed on Bermudian sail.*

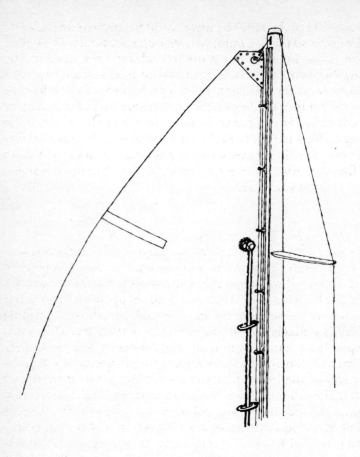

*Top end of mainsail downhaul (see previous page).*

dangerous situation and one which is not uncommon. If a man by himself is not quite certain that his boat does not suffer from this malaise he should rig the gear necessary to overcome it.

A light Terylene line should be passed through an eyelet let into the luff tabling at a level with, or just below, the upper spreader and this line should be long enough to reach the deck on each side of the sail. The line should be knotted on each side of the eyelet so that it cannot pass through. It should be fastened to the sail at intervals down the luff tabling with small plastic spring hooks to prevent it from flying free and fouling with other gear. If the sail jams, the single-hander can free the line from the bottom few hooks, take it to a halyard winch and force the sail down. He may need a snatch block to make a lead or the line may lead naturally to the halyard winch. He can use this gear on either side of the sail depending on the tack he is on. He will find that after a few feet, once the sail is free of the spreaders, it will come down easily.

## Reefing down wind

It must be possible to reef the mainsail without rounding into the wind. Roller reefing often needs another hand to pull the leech of the sail out along the boom so that it does not wrinkle when the boom is turned. This may not happen for the first few turns where the leech of the sail is roped, but above the roping the sail is unlikely to roll properly unless attended. This is unacceptable for a man by himself. Sometimes the sail can be persuaded to roll neatly by screwing lengths of tapered wood to the after end of the boom to adjust its thickness but with a strong wind in the sail the leech is likely to be turned in when the boom is rolled so that the reefed sail does not set properly. If roller reefing is found to be practicable the worm and pinion gear is more powerful and easier to use than the ratchet type, which is nevertheless sometimes found in quite large yachts. With roller reefing the lower batten pockets must be parallel to the boom, otherwise the single-hander will have to take the lower battens out of the sail before he can reef.

Point or slab reefing is, in the last analysis, simplest, easiest to use and most reliable. When not in use the reefing tackle along the boom can be attached with a spring clip to a short length of strong shock cord, screwed into the boom near the end to keep it from hanging loose and fouling gear on the deck when the yacht is put about. The same clip can be used to attach the tackle to an eye spliced in the end of the reef pendant. A single-hander

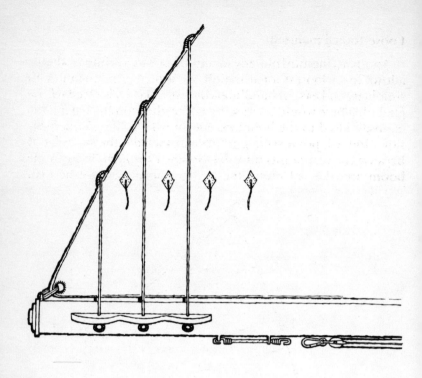

*Clew reef pendants for first, second and third reefs.*

should make sure that the pendants pass easily through the holes in the reef comb. If bee blocks are not used these holes should be sleeved with copper pipe turned over at top and bottom. The great advantage of point reefing for a man alone is that the reef can be taken in with the sail fully out: even if the points themselves cannot be tied at once, the sail will be quickly and efficiently shortened. As the reefed sail will be held only by the pendant at the clew, it is wise to tie a preventer line through the cringle and round the boom and then slack the pendant tackle until the strains are even.

## Loose-footed mainsail

Another, inestimable advantage of points reefing is that it allows for a loose-footed mainsail – a further contributor to simplicity and ease of handling which the man by himself will be glad of. There would seem to be no justification for having the mainsail laced to the boom except to make roller reefing possible. Indeed, point reefing is made awkward if the sail is laced because the reef points must be threaded through between the boom and the sail under the lacing before they can be tied.

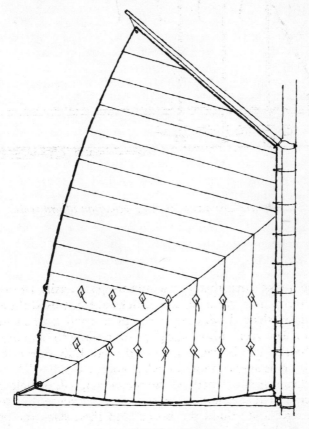

*Loose-footed mainsail.*

Lacing does not significantly support the weight of the boom, neither does it hold the sail in a better aerodynamic set. In fact, lacing usually distorts the shape of the sail, tending to pull the sail into a pocket or bulge along the boom. A loose-footed sail will hang in an easy curve along the foot and allow the air to flow naturally. It can equally be employed with Bermudian or gaff rig but it precludes the use of roller reefing. With a loose-footed sail the tack can be triced up to give a clear view for'ard in crowded waters.

**Mitre cut**

If the sail is to be loose footed its cut should be carefully considered by the single-hander when it is ordered from the sailmaker. The strongest and most efficient way to cut a loose footed sail for a cruising yacht, whether it be gaff or Bermudian, is with a mitre seam from the clew to the luff of the sail – this seam bisects the angle between the leech and the foot. In this way any extra weight borne by the clew because the sail is loose footed, will be taken along the seam so that the actual cloths will not be pulled out of shape. A mitre cut sail gives the best of all worlds because the cloths drop vertically down to the foot and run out to the leech at right angles. In this way a good roach can be cut into the leech and the foot without the need for sail battens. A mitre cut sail will not pull out of shape when it gets old but care should be taken when the sail is being made that it does not have "tightness" along the mitre seam – otherwise the sail will be drawn up across its belly and its set will be spoiled. A sail cut in this way is less liable to chafe because the seams near the mast will lie up and down instead of across the stays when the sail is fully out.

**Restitching**

Terylene sails are liable to tear along the seams when they begin to age because the stitches stand proud out of the cloth instead of being embedded in the material as in a canvas sail. After a maximum of five years, or if the sail shows signs of wear, an additional line of stitching should be sewn into the centre of each seam. This may save the single-hander the considerable labour of sewing across his mainsail by hand if the stitching gives way at sea. If he does have to restitch a seam he should use an ordinary round stitch but he should place the stitches in the same needle holes as are already in the material. It is easier to use ordinary Terylene twine as normally used for whippings (size 4 beeswax treated) rather than machining twine which is too fine to work easily by hand. The seams must be sewn on one side and then the sail turned and sewn on the other. This can be a major operation in the case of a mainsail, the sail may have to be unbent from the spars. The greatest wear and tear on seams and indeed on the whole sail comes in a calm when the sail is shaking and slatting and not when it is full of wind. It is kinder to the mainsail to take it down in a calm and easier on the single-hander's nerves.

Shortening sail is a task the single-hander will become well used to on a long passage and he will soon find short cuts in the handling of his gear. Each will have his own carefully rehearsed routine for reefing but it should be borne in mind that simplicity is of great value. Reefing is always done against rising bad weather, usually in a hurry, sometimes in wet, cold, conditions when the single-hander has either just woken up or is anxious to go to sleep. It is not always easy and is sometimes dangerous. Recalcitrant gear will soon wear at the edges of his temper. He must prepare every step in strict sequence according to a well thought out plan and he must include into his routine his safety harness as an essential item.

## Cutter rig

He will find that small sails are very much easier to use than large sails and he would do well to have his rig cut to manageable proportions. A big sail like a mast-head genoa or a spinnaker, is a fine thing if a man has two or three companions, but struggling on the foredeck alone with acres of Terylene in a freshening breeze is a refinement of torture. Big sails are not only difficult to handle on the foredeck but they are equally difficult for a man by himself to fold neatly and stow in the locker. Terylene is a slippery, uncomfortable material to handle even in small areas.

The cutter rig may be the best for a man by himself where the jib can be on a self-furling gear and the staysail hanked to a stay and therefore easily controlled. There is no reason why big sails should not be used for getting the best from the boat in light airs but they should never be set flying. A boat with a bowsprit can carry a huge headsail, setting from the mast head to the bowsprit end to well abaft the shrouds but it must run up the fore stay on hanks. The stay can be arranged with an outhaul so that it can be brought in to the fore deck for the sail to be hanked on and then

*A big headsail on bowsprit end must be on a stay. The stay itself can be brought inboard for sail changing.*

sent out before the sail is hoisted. The single-hander must keep a weather eye on the sky and the barometer when flying his big sails – he will have his hands full when he comes to get them in if the breeze has freshened.

For his everyday fare at sea the single-hander will want small sails that can be set and taken in quickly and easily and tucked away neatly in the locker. A jib and a staysail together may give the same area as a single genoa, but the two smaller sails together will be more than twice as easy to handle as the one big one.

## Storm sails

The storm trysail is a sail much used by a man alone – it gives a feeling of security which allows him to rest calmly in bad weather. Even if his boat is not making as much speed as she would with a reefed main, the storm trysail will keep her jogging along until better times return and it frees the single-hander of anxiety in a strong blow. Being loose-footed and boomless it is an easy sail to handle even in a gale and if it is provided with points it can be reduced to a manageable size in all but the most furious weather. In a Bermudian rig the trysail will be set on the same track and with the same halyard that is used for the mainsail. If possible it should be given its own "siding" at the bottom of the mast so that the trysail slides can be put onto the track without taking the mainsail slides off. When the main is lowered and the trysail hoisted, "points" are opened in the main track so that the slides from the "siding" run into it. Without this arrangement it is a labour to take the main slides off the track and then put them on again each time the trysail is used. With a "siding" the trysail can be left bent on for as long as bad weather is about, even if it is not used continuously.

In a gaff-rigged boat which has no mast track, a storm trysail should be attached to the mast by parrels and beads, like the parrel on the gaff jaws. Each should be fastened round the mast individually with a toggle and eye. They should be long enough to pass outside the throat halyard which can be left in position. Alternatively, lacing can be used, but this will be more laborious to fasten each time the storm trysail is set.

133

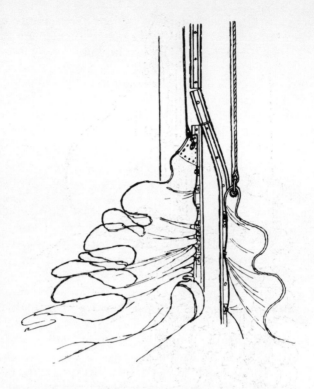

*Sliding track for the storm trysail and its slides.*

## Yawls and ketches

A two-masted rig has great advantages for a single-hander for the same reason, that sail can be split into smaller areas. Ketches are usually larger than the ideal single-handed boat but the yawl rig has several attractions. The mizen should be big enough and strongly enough stayed to carry an effective area of sail. On a reach or a quartering wind, a mizen staysail is a most excellent instrument giving great drive and great ease of handling without the risk of chafe. There should be three positions for the tack so that it can be set well out towards the rail as well as on the centre

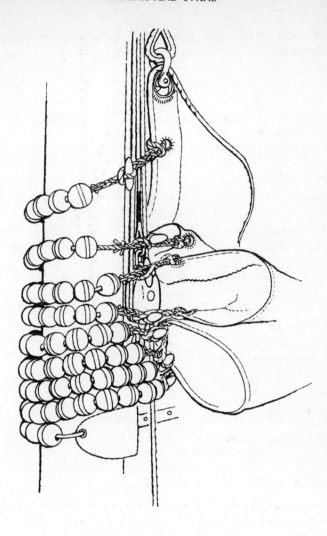

*Storm trysail ready for hoisting on a gaff rigged boat.*
*The balls on the lanyards called "parrell beads" pass*
*outside the throat halyard.*

line of the yacht depending on the wind direction. In the trades, a yacht will sail well with mizen staysail and twins alone. The mizen is also invaluable when hove-to, often giving a balance which cannot otherwise be obtained. At anchor with a strong weather-going tide a mizen will help the yacht to lie quietly. Balanced on the mizen truck is an excellent position for a radar reflector otherwise an awkward, although essential, piece of equipment to fly. Not least among its virtues, the mizen makes a good after support for a sun awning.

A man going away by himself might profitably spend a morning on the mooring looking round the deck and deciding for himself how he is going to do the many jobs by himself that he is normally helped with. Habit is an insidious master, difficult to shake free of. Often the way we approach a problem or a job on board, is dictated more by how it has been done before than by any rational and clearly thought out strategy. The modifications a boat requires in order to be easy to sail single-handed are for the most part simple, common sense adaptations of what is already on board. The most useful tool a single-hander has in his armoury is his own ability to break habit and to use his imagination.

# 10 CHOICE OF RIG

Just as square rig suffered a sudden halt to its development with the introduction of steam and motor power, so the gaff rig was abandoned by yacht designers when the new materials that made the modern Bermudian rig possible came into general use. In the period between the wars many hundreds of fine vessels had their gaffs and bowsprits torn from them and instead, tall, spindley masts erected making slow, unhandy hulks out of fine yachts. There is no more pathetic sight than an old cutter, proud and sound in all her timbers, cut down and defiled by the Bermudian rig – it was as much an insult to the rig itself, perverting it to a purpose it was never meant to serve. Instead of recognizing that the gaff rig has its place in the sailing register and devoting a proportion of their intelligence towards its development and improvement, yacht designers followed each other like drunken sheep in a headlong rush to wipe the honest gaff from the seas. They failed, not because of their own lack of zeal, but because the advantage of the gaff rig for cruising boats are so manifest and obvious that ordinary people were prepared to defy them. Now, after untold damage, the climate of opinion is changing. Modern cruising yachts are once again being designed with gaffs and bowsprits. Even some yacht designers, gifted with forward looking minds and imaginative intelligences, are turning their attention towards improving the gaff rig and applying modern technology and materials to it, as they were applied to the Bermudian. Under the relentless pressure of events, the square rigger, that astonishing pinnacle of nineteenth century inventiveness, is, at last, finding its way back to the drawing boards.

The single-hander who finds himself in possession of a gaff rigged yacht need not despair. She may be as easy to handle as a Bermudian boat and although she may not sail quite so close to the wind, she will probably be more comfortable and faster when running.

A man by himself will not spend more time than he can help beating to windward. If a cruising yacht is able to tack through 100 degrees to windward, she is performing up to average. At this rate to windward at five knots a lone sailor will do well if he makes 50 miles a day in the right direction. No one unless he is forced to, or unless he is out to prove some theory or break some record, will be happy to suffer this punishment for so small a gain. Sailing to windward in rough seas is hard on a man and his boat. The single-hander who is concerned for his own and his boat's well-being will prefer to sail a little extra distance perhaps and visit an extra harbour or so, for the sake of a fair wind. He may then be happy that his boat carries a gaff rig.

## Some advantages of a gaff

When running, the gaff sail presents a better conformation to the wind than the Bermudian sail – it is wider at the top and nearer in shape to a square sail, which is the optimum. When the yacht is rolling, particularly in a light air, a gaff will hold the sail steady so that it will present its real shape to the wind. Wind speed is greater at the top of the mast than it is at deck level. A Bermudian sail has proportionately its greatest area at the bottom thus the top of the sail is narrowest where it needs to be widest. For this reason, a gaff rigged boat is likely to be more efficient down wind although the mast may not be quite so high. The narrow top part of a Bermudian sail, unsupported laterally, is often useless because the wind power it does contain is shaken out of it by the rolling of the ship. A gaff rigged boat is also likely to roll less than a Bermudian because the sail is wider at the top of the mast and therefore has a greater steadying effect. If a topsail is set these advantages are considerably increased. A topsail puts sail where it is needed, at the top of the mast and at right angles to it.

## A modern gaff

It is argued that the gaff rig is clumsy, inefficient and makes for heavy handling and hard work but with good design these arguments are invalid. The gaff on a 30ft boat need not be a heavy spar – if it is made of ash, or any light strong wood and is approximately 15ft long it can be lifted with one hand – if made of alloy even lighter. Equally, the boom of a well-designed gaff rig should not project out over the stern any more than with Bermudian rig – this is old fashioned and unnecessary. On a gaff rigged boat in normal conditions both halyards are hauled together with no undue strain and if both have the same number of parts the sail will go up evenly. If throat and peak are raised separately the weight on either is less than on an equivalent area of Bermudian sail. If both halyards are of rope the falls may be very long owing to the purchase required and a nuisance to coil and stow, but there is no reason why gaff sails should not be hoisted on wires from halyard winches. If this were done, throat and peak could each be hoisted on a single part of wire as is a modern Bermudian sail. There have been gaff rigged boats successfully rigged in this way. Topsails can also be made aerodynamically efficient. Laurent Giles & Partners designed a topsail for *Dyarchy* where the luff rope feeds itself into a groove in the mast at the hounds and sets as snug against the mast as a dinghy sail.

The single-hander with gaff rig should find it easy to set and take in the mainsail in a strong following wind, but he will need extra gear – vangs from the end of the gaff, one on each side of the sail and double topping lifts. Two topping lifts are needed because in a gaff sail this rope passes across the middle of the sail. When handing this sail, the leeward topping lift will foul unless it is taken clear. They should be on spring clips or some other quick release gear so that the leeward one can be let go from the boom and stowed out of the way in the shrouds. If they

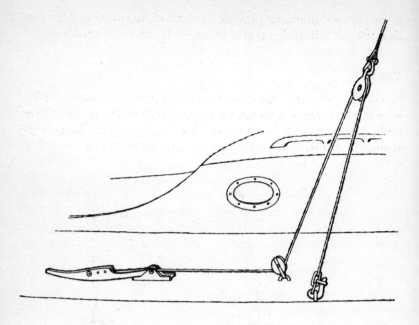

*Running backstay with Highfield lever and quick
release fastening for completely clearing lee deck.*

are clipped to a strop at the end of the boom instead of to the
spar itself, the clips can be reached more easily from the deck by
grasping the strop and pulling it inboard. They can both be
tightened by the same downhaul to which they should also be
attached by spring clips. In this way the lee topping lift can be
cleared right away from the sail so that it cannot impede
hoisting or lowering.

It is also necessary to clear the runners from the lee deck when
hoisting or lowering sail, as well as to avoid chafe. If Highfield
levers are fitted some sort of quick release fastening should be
used on the standing leg of the runner strop so that a man by
himself can slip it, even if the sail is pressed against it. It is good
practice both in gaff and Bermudian boats for the after shroud

to be encased in plastic pipe or, better still, in wooden rollers so that the sail will slide up and down easily and without chafe.

## Vangs

The purpose of vangs is to control the gaff when the mainsail is being hoisted or lowered in a seaway when the yacht will be rolling heavily and, in addition to act as lazy jacks. The vangs should be led so that when the sail is set, they fall from the end of

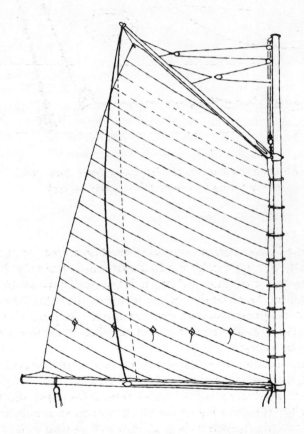

*Vangs, port and starboard, to control the gaff*

141

the gaff to a block or deadeye attached to the boom at the point where the end of the gaff lies when the sail is furled. From the deadeye the lead should be for'ard to a jam cleat, one on each side for each vang, screwed to the for'ard end of the boom. It is important to control the gaff when the sail is being hoisted and lowered. It may catch the single-hander a heavy blow if it is allowed to swing violently back and forth as well as making it difficult to move freely about the deck. If the vangs are led correctly and used correctly the most vicious gaff can be rendered docile. An advantage of the gaff is that it lessens the likelihood of an accidental gybe because the sail is held rigid at the top. It also does away with the need for sail battens.

Hoisting the mainsail in a strong trade wind for a man by himself is an operation that requires careful planning. Once the tiers are off and everything is cleared away on the lee side of the sail the vangs should be let free and at the same time the peak hoisted until the gaff is resting against the lee shroud. Then both halyards should be hauled together but the boom should be left on the gallows with the sheet hauled tight until enough sail is set to keep the boom steady against the yacht's roll. Then the single-hander should adjust his vane steering to counteract the increased weather helm the mainsail will produce, ease away a few feet on the main sheet and make it fast, then heave the boom clear of the gallows with the weather topping lift. The sail should then go up easily.

## Dropping the peak

In a squall, when the yacht may suddenly be overpressed, the peak in a gaff rigged yacht can be dropped, effectively spilling wind out of the sail and halving the area. Provided the weight of the boom is supported by the topping lift no harm will come to the sail. The top half will fall behind the bottom half in a line from the throat to the clew. If the sail is pressed against the shrouds on a run, it may be necessary to pull the top of the gaff down by using the weather vang and this can be done at the same time as the peak halyard is slacked so that control is kept over the gaff at all times. It is not good practice to sail for long periods with the peak fully dropped because extra strain is put on the throat of the sail which will carry more weight without the help of the peak halyard.

## Shortening sail

More often, the mainsail will have to be taken off in a strong following wind. Although twin staysails may be standard rig for the trades the single-hander will often find that he needs his mainsail because the wind has fallen light. Very often the mainsail will be hoisted and both twins left in position against an increase in wind later in the day. The temptation, as the wind freshens, is to leave the mainsail up for longer than is prudent – then it must be taken down in a hard wind. This must be done with great care for fear of a standing gybe – a greater danger for a man working without a helmsman.

As the mainsail is taken off, the balance on the self-steering gear will be altered and the yacht will bear away. While tending the halyards the single-hander must keep an eye to the burgee and as soon as the wind begins to creep round the weather quarter, he must leave the halyards and run aft to adjust the self-steering. The halyards should be let go a few feet and the sail pulled down, the peak with the weather vang which should be hauled in a bit at a time and jammed on its cleat, the throat by physically pulling down the luff of the sail, or by a downhaul on the gaff jaws. As the sail comes down the sheet should be hauled in and the vane adjusted as the twins take over. The vang will be kept tight as the gaff falls until it is two blocks and the gaff is resting on top of the boom. Then the lee vang can be hauled in so as to gather up the folds of the sail and the end of the weather vang used as a sail tier to make a neat stow.

## A standing gybe

In a Bermudian yacht the mainsail may be more difficult to get down when full of wind. The top battens may have to be sacrificed if they foul themselves over the crosstrees. The sheet will have to be pulled hard in to lift the sail as much as possible from the mast and the single-hander will have to watch even more carefully against a standing gybe. As the gear is lighter in a Bermudian boat and the sail narrower at the top and unrestrained by a gaff the wind may get behind it as the yacht rolls. This may be enough to induce a gybe if she is even slightly by the lee. A standing gybe in a strong wind with twins set and the mainsail half down, will produce immediate chaos. Even if no sail is torn and no damage is done to the runner, the yacht will immediately broach – she may even be knocked down – the weather twin will go aback and she will lose her way and lie helpless in the trough.

Having first ascertained that he himself is still in one piece the single-hander will have to set about repairing the effect of a standing gybe in the ocean and get the boat back on course. The mainsail, pinned in, will be full of wind heeling the yacht over and forcing her to windward. The weather twin will be aback and will effectively stop her way. The lee twin will be flapping wildly shaking the mast and tearing at its sheet, its boom trailing in the water. This is the moment for the man alone to muster his calm – it is the moment when his experience alone will teach him to think clearly and act wisely. The yacht will be in irons and it may not be easy to get her out of it without damage.

## Quick release runners

If the mainsail is hard against the runner it will not come down unless the runner can be let go. This may not be easy if every part of it is bar tight. Clearly the sail which is doing most damage, either actually or potentially, should be taken down first – perhaps the lee twin. Then the runner must somehow be loosened so that the main sheet can be let out, giving the yacht some chance to pay off. If the runners are controlled by a tackle, this can be overhauled and the runner taken to the shrouds. It is much safer to have a quick release slip-shackle on the bottom of a runner tackle so that, in case of need, the whole affair can be cleared quickly even if it has strain on it. This applies to a rope runner tackle and to the wire strop of a Highfield lever.

Once the mainsail has been freed the yacht may pay off of her own accord – if she has a bowsprit she can be helped by breaking out the jib furling gear and pulling the sheet a-weather. It may be necessary to lower the other twin, even to start the engine, before she will come back on course.

If this misfortune happens in a gaff rigged boat the topping lift will also have to be changed before the mainsail can be taken down. This is a major disadvantage of gaff rig in the ocean. A standing gybe is one of the most dangerous accidents that can happen to a single-hander and is capable of breaking a runner, breaking the main boom, tearing a sail, carrying away the boom gallows or doing some more serious damage. When it comes it is often without warning which makes its effect the more

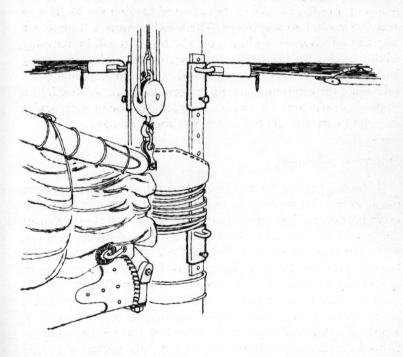

*Spare track slide* (lower right) *to facilitate mainsail hoops being hoisted past twin running sails.*

145

devastating. It is usually the product of that most ancient of vices – carrying too much sail on a run and it can be guarded against only by vigilance, caution and care.

A feature of gaff rig is the lack of a mast track and slides – an advantage in some respects which is paid for in others. Instead, a gaff sail has hoops or a lacing to hold the luff to the mast. Hoops are notorious for getting themselves jammed aloft and refusing to come down. Sometimes a light line is rigged up from the bottom hoop, clove hitched to the for'ard part of each one so that they can be pulled clear of the mast from below. A luff lashing is preferable to hoops provided it is correctly rove, not round and round the mast but to each eyelet and back round the mast to the next and so on to the bottom of the sail. To reef the sail with points reefing it is not necessary to cast off this lashing or hoops, but if roller reefing is fitted this must be done. Hoops or lashings are equally inconvenient when running with twin staysail booms set in tracks on the sides of the mast, because the booms prevent the mainsail from passing up or down the mast when setting or reefing or taking it in — the price to be paid for not having a mast track. Here again the single-hander must improvise, having no one to hold the booms clear while the mainsail is being hauled up or down past the inboard ends of the twin staysail booms. A spare ringed track slide should be used which should be fed into the top of the track when the mainsail is being lowered and the bottom when it is hoisted, the heels of the booms being moved from one ring to the other past the hoops or lashing or the gaff jaws.

## Climbing aloft

Mast hoops are useful for climbing aloft, which the single-hander may have to do for any number of reasons. This is not easy in a seaway for a man by himself. Some yachts have ratlines or wooden rungs up the lower shrouds but these will not serve to climb above the hounds. A man alone can haul himself aloft in a bos'n's chair if he first sends one end of a tackle up the mast on his main halyard or topmast gant line. It should be a double purchase or at least a luff tackle or he will be exhausted when he gets to the top and may be unable to work efficiently. If nothing else is available, the main sheet, with its blocks may be used for this purpose. The motion aloft in the ocean is very violent and dangerous for a man swinging about in a chair, especially if he has no one to tend him. Unless in a dire emergency the single-hander should leave jobs aloft for in harbour. If it is imperative to go aloft he should first settle the yacht on a course which gives her the least motion and then rig a preventer from the top of the chair lines to the mast or one of the stays, or even shackle the top of the chair to a stay. The preventer should not be rigged from the chair itself as the single-hander will be jerked out of his senses. Even with a preventer he will be hurled from side to side with great force and will be lucky if he does not injure himself. The chair lines should be as short as possible so that the ring or shackle holding them is in the single-hander's lap when he is sitting in the chair. A bight of the fall of the tackle or halyard, should be taken through the ring, over the single-hander's head and body and under the chair. In this way he can pull himself aloft a little at a time, easing the rope through the ring at every pull, and if he should suddenly release his hold on the halyard he will not fall to the deck. He should bear in mind that it is dangerous to go aloft in a seaway – the job must be done slowly, with care and with every possible precaution against accident. Going aloft in a seaway is always dangerous. A further tip is to leave a sail set: this gives something for the man aloft to be cushioned against if thrown in a heavy roll. Try a weight on the end of the hauling part, which is then thrown overboard so it cannot foul other gear.

## Value of a topsail

The topsail is one of the most useful sails in the single-hander's locker. If it is a thimble-headed sail, without jackyard, it can be set very easily and quickly. On a run it immediately eases the motion of a yacht in the ocean and gives her extra speed. It is even worth setting the topsail over the reefed mainsail when it will serve to ease rolling and will not overpress the yacht. Jackyarder topsails may not find favour with a single-handed cruising man because of their clumsiness and the difficulty of stowing the yard easily when the sail is not in use but a thimble headed topsail is a joy. It is one of the great advantages of gaff rig. For his every day fare at sea the single-hander will want small sails that can be set and taken in quickly and easily and that can be tucked away neatly in the locker. A jib and a staysail together may give the same area as a single genoa foresail, but two smaller sails will be more than twice as easy to handle.

All this gear which is associated with the gaff rig is well tried and tested and has been handed down by generation after generation of sailors although not in connection with single-handed sailing which has become popular only in recent times. The modern single-hander, using traditional gear, will have to make his own improvements and modifications as he goes along using any methods he finds to hand, ancient or modern. There is no room for purism or traditionalism in single-handed sailing.

Setting sails and taking them in, reefing sails, changing sails and altering the trim of sails is the single-hander's life. If he is to get the best out of his boat and make a reasonable fast passage across the ocean he must be at it the whole time. Hardly a day passes, even in the steadiest of trade winds, when some movement does not have to be made to a sail and often this process is almost continuous, changes in wind strength and direction following one another so quickly that the single-hander has his work cut out to keep up with them. Each job, whether it be setting or taking in twin staysails or storm trysail or topsail or genoa foresail will have its own carefully ordered sequence and its own neatly worked out drill. It is surprisingly hard work for a man alone and takes more than twice as long as it would take two men working together. When conditions are bad and sails have to be reefed and taken in, perhaps at night when the fore deck is a remote, lonely place, unfriendly and alien to the cosy cabin, the task is daunting to the bravest heart. Then the lone sailor will be glad that he has the routine at his finger tips and can move silently and methodically from halyard to guy to winch to cleat until the job is done and he feels his boat once more comfortable and within herself.

# 11 FOOD AND DRINK AND THINGS

There are countless things a man must take with him on a voyage by himself and countless more things that may not be essential to his survival but which will help him to overcome the difficulties, disasters, alarms and emergencies which he is likely to meet. There are things for the running of the ship, things for his own personal happiness and things to drink and eat. His aim must be to have as little of everything as is acceptable and as much of everything as is possible, a balance which is as hard to define as it is to achieve.

Above all, he must know where everything in his boat is to be found – the virtue of tidiness, if he does not possess it when his voyage starts, will be forced on the single-hander by the pressures of his everyday life. He must be able to reach his hand immediately for what he urgently needs, by day or in the dark, in the certain knowledge that it has been put back in its proper place – his safety depends on this. Whether it is a spanner or a spike or a sail needle or a parbuckle strop it is useless unless the single-hander knows where it is.

## The stores list

The single-hander has an advantage in having plenty of space in which to stow what he needs or what he believes he may need. His danger will not be that he has too few but that he has too many things, so that when he needs to find some item that is

149

on board and which he knows is, he cannot find it. Lockers in boats tend to silt from the bottom upwards so that on a long voyage the single-hander will forget exactly what he has and where it is to be found. A permanent, stiff covered note-book is vital for this purpose as well as for many others. Each locker and each part of the ship which is used for stowage, should be listed as it is filled with gear.

As far as is possible spare gear should be stowed logically. For instance, all materials for mending leaks in the hull – sheet lead, copper, fibreglass cloth, old inner tubes, strips of canvas, large copper nails and galvanized nails, a bag of mixed sand and cement, should all be together in one place and listed accord-ingly. Spare parts for cooking stoves, primus, pressure cooker rings and valves and pressure plugs, blow lamp or primus prickers and parts, gas adaptors and spare hose, pump washers, lamp wicks and glasses, should be listed and put in one specific place. Electrical spares – bulbs, fuses, flex, strip solder, in-sulating tape should have a large tin or a box to themselves and a place in the note-book. The bos'n's box should include waxed Terylene twine, natural fibre twine, spike, fid, serving mallet, whipping and seizing twine, scissors, beeswax, needles in a small pot of Vaseline, strips of Terylene and canvas and stick-on patches.

The best type of serving mallet for a single-hander is one which carries its own twine on a small reel so that no other person is needed to pass the twine when serving a wire or rope.

## The tool chest

Tools should be in a dry convenient and accessible place – they are needed more frequently than anything else on board and should be given the best possible stowage. In addition to the ordinary run of hammer, chisels, screw-drivers, bradawl, spanners and hacksaws, the kit should include a vice as well as drills, brace and bits, coarse and fine and round files, at least a Surform plane if no proper plane is carried and a saw kit with different types of blade fitting a single handle. There should be tools for jobs in metal and for jobs in wood like joining a broken spar, covering a split hatch, repairing a tiller or a pump handle. A good supply of two-part glue should be carried, both quick and slow setting and quantities of glass cloth and resin as well as ordinary adhesives, fillers, pipe bandages and Jubilee clips of all sizes. The man alone needs a good variety of clamps in various shapes and sizes so that jobs can be held in position when working alone.

Engine tools and spanners are another department. As well as basics such as spare sparking plugs or injectors, enough spanners and gaskets and valves should be carried even if a major overhaul is beyond the skill of the single-hander. In some remote part, he will for certain meet a friend who can do the job, provided he has the spares and tools. The exhaust system of an engine is highly vulnerable and a good supply of exhaust bandage and exhaust sealer and tin patches to be fastened with Jubilee clips must be carried. Somewhere on board a strong magnet should be stowed – for fishing in the bilges and under the engine.

There should be a wood store on board with a quantity of hard wood and soft wood in various lengths and sections such as $2 \times 1$ inches, $2 \times 2$ inches and $\frac{3}{4} \times 6$ inches planks stowed in the bilges or behind cockpit lockers in as long lengths as is practicable. There must be spare screws, steel and brass, nails, bolts of various sizes, which should always be threaded right up, and a wide variety of nuts, washers and odds and ends saved from a thousand jobs to come in useful at some future time.

Spare sails and rope and awnings are a part of every yacht's equipment. The single-hander would be wise to include a long, strong and flexible rope which can be used as a hawser in case either of towing or being towed. It is useful to carry a small portable electric sewing machine for repairing or altering or making new sails or awnings.

## Water and fuel consumption

All spare gear, together with details of food stowage should be listed at one end of the note-book together with its location, unless, of course, this is obvious. In another part of the book the single-hander should keep a record of fresh water taken on board at each port and at what date, so that a check can be kept of consumption. Similarly, and perhaps as important, there should be a record of fuel taken on board together with the number of engine hours run. These simple statistics are interesting in themselves, perhaps after the voyage is over, and they may be helpful to the single-hander himself or to others. In the same note-book the chronometer log can be kept and a list of all the charts carried on board. These should be arranged in order of use and each one given a consecutive number which should be pencilled in on the chart so that new numbers can be added.

It is useful and informative to extract from the ship's log a continuous voyage record, showing the boat's performance day by day with both the actual and accumulated run and accumulated log distance, entering the mean average speed for the passage and the actual distance by traverse table between points. This information is very useful – it shows the accuracy of the patent log at a glance and the effectiveness of the courses steered. The best and the worst days progress stand out of such a list with great clarity and in retrospect it makes fascinating reading.

## Importance of food

A man must eat to live but he should beware of living only in order to eat. Food becomes important to a man alone – meals mark the passing hours and days with as much significance as the rising and setting of the sun. Eating, after all, is one of the two major preoccupations of life. The other, being in all respects absent for a man alone, he may be tempted to lean too heavily towards it. Meals are looked forward to, planned and prepared for with great care and consideration, consumed with relish and digested with deep satisfaction. Special luxuries will be saved up to celebrate special days – a birthday, the mid-point of an ocean, the sighting of a ship, the longest day's run – excuses for self-indulgence are easy to find.

Food may assume disproportionate importance in the life of a man alone – preparing food is a considerable art and consuming it a considerable pleasure. He will need restraint and self-discipline to keep both the art and its product under control. The sense of routine and order which will quickly become a part of his life will help him to do this. Nevertheless, the lone sailor should give serious thought to the type of food he is going to take with him and how it can best be stored and stowed.

## Planned stowage

The available stowage space should be clearly divided into ready-use and sea stores. The ready-use lockers should be those that are used for week-end or holiday food stowage, expanded if necessary to give enough space to last the single-hander for two or three weeks. He should first fill these lockers with the normal things that he has with him during the course of his normal sailing and then he should multiply up the quantities and stock his sea stores. The locker for sea stores need not be as accessible – if the space under the bunks is used for tins, it should be raised three or four inches from the ship's planking or lining with wooden slats, an inch or so apart, and the slats covered with plastic mesh to stop small tins falling through into the bilge. General divisions can be made for meat, fish, veg, fruit, cheese, soup, fruit-juice, salad, milk, coffee, tea and the myriad items to eat that each single-hander will wish to carry. A plan of the space should be made in the note-book and the positions of each group of items drawn in. This should be done for every locker used for sea stores. Additionally, each item should be listed in the same note-book and the number of tins, jars, bottles, etc., marked against it. If this is not done the single-hander will forget what his sea stores are and how much of each item he has. When necessary the ready-use should be replenished from the sea stores and an adjustment made in the note book.

If there is any danger of bilge water in these lockers paper labels must be taken off the tins, which should then be identified by waterproof marker. Loose tin labels floating in the bilges are guaranteed to block the pump intake whenever it is wanted in an emergency. The single-hander will also be in danger of eating peaches instead of carrots with his beef roll. Packet food must be wrapped in polythene bags and stowed in dry lockers but all dry packet food must be looked at frequently, particularly in hot weather. Some cereal-based packet food contains micro-organisms which in warm weather take on a new and vigorous life so that suddenly, the single-hander may find his boat alive with small creatures. Tins are a great convenience, enabling him to get himself a palatable, hot meal quickly, but he will not wish to live on tins exclusively. Dehydrated vegetables keep a higher proportion of their natural food value than tinned products and lend themselves to more imaginative cooking. They are economical of space, but, of course, they require larger amounts of water.

The single-hander planning a long voyage will be wise to start his venture with full lockers. At home, before he starts, he will be able to get the food he is used to and the food he knows is reliable, probably more cheaply than in foreign parts. His food lockers are an investment – they are an absolute guarantee against inflation. He should keep them full by living off his ready-use and replenishing his sea stores at every opportunity.

With careful purchasing, it is possible to carry enough fresh food for all but the longest passages. Vegetables, eggs, butter, cheese and some fruit will all keep, without refrigeration, for thirty days or more if carefully bought and properly stowed. Soft, tropical fruits do not as a general rule keep as well as citrus, of which a good supply should be carried.

Limes or lemon juice, sweetened with honey, is a delicacy. Oranges, either for juice or for eating, will last for weeks. Bananas can be graded when bought to ripen over a long period. If they are brought aboard by the stalk or hand they should be dipped in the sea for several minutes before stowing, otherwise the ship will become infested with small flying insects.

It is infinitely better to buy fresh provisions direct from the producer than from any shop. Enquiries ashore will usually lead to some small market gardener outside the town who will be more than willing to supply the bulk of the single-hander's vegetables direct from the ground and for those that he cannot supply, he will have a friend or acquaintance who will. It is usually better to provision the ship in a small port rather than a large – although the variety may be less generous, goods are usually fresher and cheaper.

## Vegetable stowage

Vegetables should not be washed before they are stored but surplus greenery should be taken off – radishes and spring onions and carrots store better this way. They should not be buried in some deep, damp bilge or shovelled wholesale into a locker, but placed in small wooden crates or baskets in a position where there is ample air circulation but not too much light. They should be inspected every day and any that show the first signs of deterioration should be removed and either eaten or thrown away. Potatoes and root vegetables will keep in this way for long periods. Cabbage is a most pleasing vegetable – if it is reasonably young it will keep for several weeks. Apart from steamed, shredded and used raw in salads, it is delectable when marinated and will serve the single-hander for valuable roughage in his diet. The onion is another vegetable that will last the duration of most single-handed voyages. It is so obviously versatile and beneficial that no man alone will consider going to sea without an adequate supply. Even tomatoes can be made to last for many days if they are carefully graded and taken from the locker as they ripen. Rot spreads very quickly from one vegetable to another and must be weeded out immediately it is observed.

## Protein source

Beans can form an excellent staple for a man by himself – there are a great variety of them, and can be stowed easily in bottles or plastic jars where they will keep for months. They are an excellent source of protein – better than tinned meat or fish – and they are very good eating if cooked tastefully. There are many varieties of beans – cooking them is an art worth cultivating for the single-hander. They vary in hardness from soya beans, which need twenty five to thirty minutes at 15 lb pressure, down to Great Northerns, kidney beans, whole peas, red beans, black beans, garbanzos (chickpeas), brown beans, Lima beans, pink beans, pinto beans, navy beans (haricots), split peas, black eyed peas and lentils which are the softest and only require six to ten minutes' pressure cooking. There is no end to the delights of the simple bean – an excellent book is *Bean Cuisine*, published by Routledge and Kegan Paul of 39 Store Street, London W.C.1.

The single-hander will need a pressure cooker to get the best out of beans and, indeed, his cooking will benefit greatly from this indispensable piece of galley equipment. It is economical on fuel, preserves the nutrients in his food, saves water, and enables him to cook his meal on one burner in no more than a few minutes.

### Keeping food cool

A man alone can manage comfortably, even in tropical waters, without refrigeration. Whether operated by electricity or gas, refrigerators are an unending source of worry. They may be essential equipment for a charter yacht but, on balance, the single-hander is probably better off without. If electric, an efficient refrigerator uses an unacceptable amount of battery power, making it necessary to run the engine or generator every day. If gas, there is a constant danger that the flame will be blown out or extinguished in some way, so that gas is released into the bilge. At sea where it is not often unbearably hot for long periods, the problem is minimal. Butter and ready-use food can be kept cool in an earthenware dish with a water jacket operating on the evaporation principle. In harbour, ice is usually available cheaply and this can be kept for up to two days in a special box or bag or in a thermos flask. It is useful to carry a thermos flask with a wide neck and a large round cork for the purpose of storing ice.

Free range eggs bought direct from the farm will keep for at least 30 days, or longer if they are covered with a thin coating of Vaseline and stowed in ordinary egg boxes. Wrapped cheese

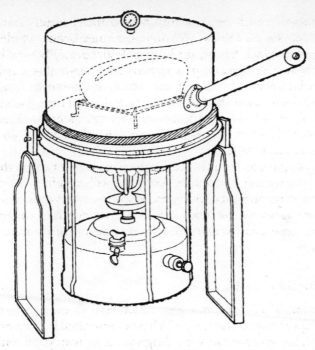

*Surface oven on simple paraffin pressure stove.*

and slightly salted butter will both keep for long periods although it is wise to take tins both of cheese and butter in the sea stores as there are many parts of the world where these commodities are expensive or even unobtainable. Nuts, raisins, sultanas, currants, dates and olives are also a natural and very acceptable source of protein and sweetness, which are all easy to store and at least in some parts of the world, inexpensive. Barley sugar can be a good companion in the night watches. In addition to coffee and tea and often more acceptable, Marmite makes a good night-time drink (it also contains vitamins of the B group) especially with crusts of bread or hard biscuit dunked.

## A simple surface oven

Bread is often considered an essential item of diet although

157

any of the rye biscuits available are a good alternative. Freshly baked wholemeal bread will keep for up to two weeks but care must be taken to keep it free of mildew. If the single-hander in a boat without an oven cares to turn his talents towards baking, he can quite easily make himself or have made a serviceable surface oven. A piece of $\frac{3}{4}$ inch iron cut into a disc about 7 inches across, or a convenient size to fit his stove, should be grooved round the edge to a depth of about $\frac{1}{4}$ inch to take an upturned steel saucepan of suitable diameter which will be the oven's lid. The handle should be cut off short, or if possible, turned the other way up so that it can be used to lift the lid off. To be sophisticated, a hole can be cut in the top of the lid and a round thermometer inserted. This surface oven can be heated on calor gas or a primus stove. It should be provided with a wire trivet to keep the bread off the bottom surface of the oven. The contraption will be found to bake excellent bread but if it is to be used at sea, the single-hander should be certain that it is properly gimballed and in all respects safe – it will get very hot and be a dangerous fire hazard if it goes adrift in a seaway while being used.

## Fresh water

Clearly, the more fresh water that can be carried the better, having regard to the fact that water is heavy and takes up a lot of space. Tanks should be in or near the bilges, amidships if possible. The man alone is well placed for water capacity as most yachts are fitted with tanks to cater for a crew. One gallon per day for drinking, washing and cooking is enough for a man who is moderate in his drinking and will provide a fair standard of cleanliness. There are ports where the drinking water is of poor quality and others where it is excellent. Tanks should be fitted with drains so that they can be emptied and better water put in when available. There should be no more than one point in the ship where fresh water can be got and it should always be by a pump and not from a tap or cock which can accidentally be left on. Apart from the ship's tanks, the single-hander should keep a large can of fresh water stowed separately so that if he should lose his main supply through a leaky tank or by some contamination, he will survive. The easiest way to collect water from a tropical downpour or ordinary rain, is by means of the sail cover hung under the boom with a bucket at the inboard end. It is sometimes wise to use a water purifier, of which there are several brands available. Beer may be a comfort to a man alone on a long passage. He should have a bottle of medicinal brandy on board.

## Sharks and poisonous fish

The single-hander can, if he wishes, supplement his diet by fishing. In higher latitudes mackerel and sometimes sea trout can be caught with a spinner by no other skill than that of being in the right place when the fish are running. In tropical waters he should be very careful because a considerable number of quite easily caught fish are virulently poisonous. If he wants to eat fresh fish he should have with him a book which describes how poisonous fish can be recognized. In tropical waters the lovely Dorado can sometimes be caught quite easily but it is usually a much bigger fish than a man alone can consume and it is a creature of such consummate beauty that the single-hander may be reluctant to kill it. Sharks often follow a yacht for long periods, especially if edible scraps are being thrown overboard. They can be caught with a large baited hook and a stout line. A man alone will interfere with these creatures at his peril. They are immensely strong, dangerous if provoked, very tough and not good to eat. They often appear dead when they are still very much alive and if brought aboard a yacht they can cause untold damage by suddenly reviving and threshing violently and very destructively. Yachts have had their cockpits and upperworks smashed almost beyond repair by a shark that had been considered dead. Flying fish can be fried and eaten – they are considered by some sailors to be a delicacy. They will come aboard a yacht at night, particularly if a light is shown and can be collected from the scuppers in the morning.

## Plankton as food

Plankton can be gathered by throwing astern a linen or dense cotton or light canvas bag open at one end like a small sea-anchor. The plankton collects quite quickly in cool weather, faster at night than by day, forming a stiff, jelly- or cake-like substance which gives off an unpleasant smell. However, it is not unpleasant to eat – something between fish paste and caviar – and it has a high calorific value. It is strong enough provender to nourish the blue whale, the world's largest animal.

After many days alone the single-hander may feel himself so much a part of the environment he finds himself in, so attuned to the changing moods and humours of the ocean, that he may not wish to interfere with its inhabitants. He himself is tolerated, even treated as a friend by the creatures with whom he shares his life. They all in their way contribute to his well-being – the flashing beauty of the flying fish, the grace and elegance of the dolphin, the deadly power of the shark, the ponderous and dignified bulk of the whale, the hurried, busy flight of the storm petrel or the deft, competent mastery of the gull as it endlessly plays the currents and eddies round the yacht – all serve to draw the single-hander closer to his surroundings. It is his ability to identify with the ocean and to become a part of its life which makes it possible for him, unlike any other creature, to survive and flourish in the ocean by himself. The substance of his existence is dependent as much on his state of mind as on his bodily health – the one is as much a part of his well-being as the other. He is a wise and generous man who passes across the ocean in peace, respecting the lives of his fellow wayfarers.

# 12 THE ULTIMATE DISASTER

The walls of a sailor's house are thin – in a wooden boat the planking may be one and a quarter inches thick, in a fibreglass boat something less than half an inch and in a steel yacht three-sixteenths. This compares favourably in thickness for size with an ocean-going ship, whose plates are unlikely to be more than $\frac{3}{4}$ inch thick. Surprisingly perhaps, it is unusual for a yacht to suffer extensive damage to her outer skin, at least when she is in deep water. Wooden yachts sometimes work, particularly in way of the mast and begin to leak dangerously along the garboard seam. This can happen through over strain when going to windward in a strong blow and a rough sea, when the downwards thrust on the mast is greatest. The single-hander, always conscious that his boat is his all, is likely to be kindly towards her. If a square yard is used for running in the trades which is not properly triced, so that it cannot easily swing laterally, it may twist the mast step which in turn will loosen floors in way and planking under.

## Serious leaking

A common cause of a serious leak is a faulty skin fitting or, much more alarming and more likely for a single-hander, because he is not keeping a proper lookout, a collision with a large and heavy baulk of timber or a floating piece of deck cargo washed overboard from a ship. Yachts have been damaged and

161

sunk by whales and they have been attacked and seriously holed by swordfish. The man alone should have a well thought-out plan of action ready in the back of his mind in case he is woken by a crash in the night and his boat immediately begins to make water.

The leak is likely to be for'ard, near the water line. If he has time he should first take way off the boat to ease pressure. If the leak is accessible from the inside he may be able to stem some of the water by stuffing in rags or clothing or a life jacket or an inflatable cushion which can then be blown up. This should give him time to rig the next expedient which should be a collision mat. Sometimes this can be done effectively by lashing a large piece of canvas such as a cockpit cover or a sail, under the ship and over the leak. If it can be hauled tight enough a bunk

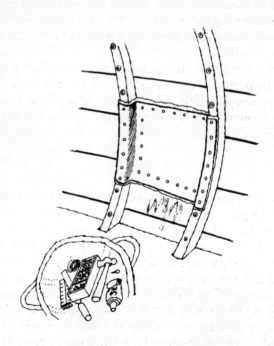

*Temporary repair with lead.*

mattress can then be forced down inside it and over the leak. With good fortune, the damage can then be repaired from the inside with a patch of sheet lead or copper. Lead is better than copper for this purpose because it takes the contour of the hull much more easily and on a wooden hull, requires nothing behind it but a thick layer of Seelastik or other gunge. It will also take copper nails without difficulty. With a fibreglass hull, lead can be fastened in place with short self-tapping screws of which a supply should be carried each with a large washer to prevent dragging through the lead. Holes must first be drilled in the skin to take the screws. With a steel hull, it may be possible to hammer the plates together or to shore the leak up from the inside using wooden struts braced against the deck-head or a bulkhead. Ordinary wooden wedges are very useful for this kind of job and should be carried on board. A strong mix of sand and cement will often stop a major leak. It should be poured into a roughly constructed wooden box over the leak – being heavy the mix will force itself into crannies that otherwise cannot be reached.

If all these devices fail him the single-hander may have to leave his boat to save his life. He should not do this until he is certain beyond doubt that the boat is sinking. Many yachts have been abandoned for lost by their crews and have then survived to confound them.

## Pumps

The single-hander who finds himself with an unmanageable leak will be greatly helped by mechanical pumps which may keep the water at bay while he attends urgently to finding and stopping it. A pump operated by the main engine should be efficient and have a high capacity. Sometimes this is achieved by switching the engine cooling water to the bilge but a simple pump working off an eccentric drive is better and usually more powerful. Apart from this mechanical pump a man by himself should have at least two efficient hand-operated pumps on board and an electric pump. One hand pump should be in the cockpit and should take the water out of the deepest part of the

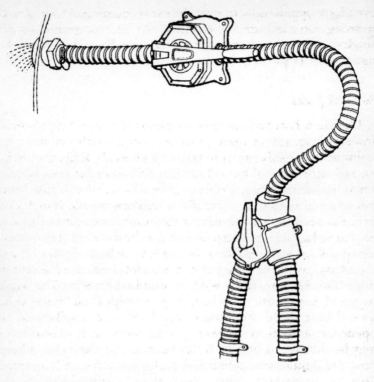

*Bilge pump with two-way cock to either port or starboard bilge.*

bilge. Another hand pump should be positioned inside the boat and should be capable of drawing from the lee bilge when the yacht is heeled. This entails a junction in the suction with one branch drawing from either bilge and a change-over cock. In this way the single-hander can drain the bilge by hand without going outside the cabin – a convenience in bad weather because it saves dressing up in wet gear. Both hand pumps should be positioned so that they are comfortable to work without twisting or contorting the body in order to reach them. In an emergency he will not have time to spend operating a pump – he may not even have opportunity to start the main engine and here, a self-priming electric pump is essential. An electric pump to the single-hander is the equivalent of a man helping him at the moment he needs help most.

## Survival packs

If all fails him and there is no means of preventing his boat from sinking, rather than go to the bottom with her the lone sailor will probably prefer to take to his life raft. Rafts should be packed with survival kit to RORC specification. It is worth the single-hander's time not only to have a list of what is inside his raft when he buys it, but actually to see the gear that is included in it. For instance, sometimes the survival kit is packed in a cloth or plastic bag which is fastened with a draw-string. This draw-string will get wet as soon as the raft is launched – it may be wet for a long period of time beforehand and it may be difficult to undo the the knot with cold or numbed fingers. The knife supplied, being inside the bag, is of no help. Equally the knife should be a sheath and not a clasp knife with a spike and an opener separate from it. Even if of stainless steel, a clasp knife may be difficult to open if it has been wet or damp for a long time. He should be certain that the raft is provided with paddles. They are important – they may make the difference between fetching some refuge or being swept away by the wind or tide, or getting clear of a fire . RORC approved survival packs, which should be in all rafts, include such things as paddles, bailer, sea anchor and flares, bellows and repair kit, but the more comprehensive pack, including a supply of water, a first-aid outfit, a fishing kit and some emergency rations is not normally packed in rafts unless specially ordered. The single-hander should also make certain that the life raft torch is really water proof and is a signalling torch.

As a supplement to the gear packed in his raft he would do well to have a small survival bag packed and ready at all times in a locker near the companion hatch or in the dog-house. In the stress of the moment of disaster basic things will be forgotten which are normally obvious – the single-hander's wallet with some money and his cheque book, a pair of trousers, a shirt and a hat, a card bearing his name, his address and the name, registered number and home port of his yacht.

## Launching the raft

The positioning of the raft and its attachment to the boat require some thought. Often it is loose in the cockpit or even inside the cabin – a bad position for a life raft. It should be in a cradle or seating strongly through-bolted to the deck and secured in the centre with a senhouse slip so that it can immediately be released. Amidships is the best position for a raft, from where it can be cast over on either side without running foul of the main sheet or the self-steering. The normal trip-line which operates the air cylinder and then becomes the raft's painter should be closely looked at by the single-hander. Often this line is of braided Terylene – strong no doubt, but almost impossible to handle in a hard wind when the raft will be tugging and pulling wildly. It should be replaced by a larger sized, preferably a natural fibre rope which can be handled in extreme conditions more easily and without damage to the hands.

## Checking raft gear

Rather than rely on having a knife ready to cut the raft free, the painter should be secured on board with a slip arrangement which can be undone from the raft after the single-hander has got into it. This can best be arranged with a peg of wood whose trip-line is long enough to reach over the side where the raft is fast. Rafts are not easy to board from the deck of a yacht in bad weather and it is essential that the raft remains attached to the yacht and close alongside after inflation, until the single-hander is actually in it. In a heavy sea it may immediately fill with water and be extremely difficult to manage for a man alone. The single-hander should also look carefully at the way the painter is secured to the raft itself – often the end of the line is simply sewn to the fabric or attached by an adhesive which may not be satisfactory.

Before a life raft is purchased he should look very carefully at what he is buying from the practical point of view of the man who may be called upon to use it by himself, probably in heavy weather. He should remember that his life raft is a "once off" piece of equipment. If he launches it and then finds that he can save his ship, he will not be able himself to repack the raft in its container. This is a job that must be done ashore in the factory.

Much of the standard survival equipment such as a whistle or a red light attached to a life jacket or a smoke float, seem to have little relevance for a man by himself. He may reason that if he falls without a harness he is doomed to drown and the act of prolonging his life by wearing a life jacket is likely only to add to his distress. On the other hand, a life jacket worn under a safety harness may be of real assistance to a man trying to heave himself back on board. The extra buoyancy can hardly be anything but a help – the fact of wearing a life jacket saves his energy in the water, which he would use to keep afloat, for the job of hauling himself aboard again. Some waterproof zip jackets are now combined with a safety harness. If these are used, care must be taken to see that the harness part is as efficient, strong and as easy to use as a harness by itself. The jacket must not be able to pull over his head under load.

### Signal flares

Of all the various pyrotechnic devices available – hand-held flares, parachute flares, rocket flares or smoke signals, the Verey pistol has advantages for the single-hander for the same reason that it is quick to use and does not commandeer his time as holding a hand flare would do. Either flares or a pistol should be in a position where they are immediately available and the cartridges or flares should be separately stowed, on the port-side of the ship for red cartridges and on the starboard side for white. The advantage of the pistol is that a white flare can be fired direct at the bridge of a ship on a dangerous course, usually with considerable effect. A Verey pistol is also a formidable defensive weapon. (It is a gun within the meaning of the Act and requires a licence in the UK.)

## Mayday calls

Most ocean-going yachts now carry VHF two-way radio which can be used for a distress call. The single-hander should remember that in a serious emergency he will be preoccupied in his efforts to save his ship and may not have time to spend in tuning and calling-up on his VHF set in order to send a Mayday signal. Conditions are likely to be bad – he himself, his gear and the whole boat may be wet and the VHF set unserviceable or impossible to operate. He may be better employed in using all his energy to get himself out of trouble than in calling for help on VHF. An automatic distress transmitter (ELT or EPIRB) may be a better device for a man alone. Its range is generally greater than VHF radio, it requires no attention after it has been started and it does not require a special aerial. This is not to say that VHF radio is not extremely useful to the single-hander. He can use it to talk to other yachts or to pass a message to a ship for onward transmission by short-wave radio. VHF is far superior for passing a message to a ship, which the single-hander may well wish to do. Sometimes when he may be late on his ETA, even overdue, it will be a comfort for him to know that his people at home are not worried for his safety. To pass a message by morse is usually difficult – even if his own signalling is good he will be lucky to find a ship that it willing and able to read morse. Shouting is impracticable unless the ship stops her engines close alongside, but most ships will be willing to send a cable for a man alone in the ocean if the message is passed to them by VHF. In some modern and congested waters VHF is almost essential for a yacht entering or leaving harbour.

Sailors are sometimes disposed to believe that in the ultimate disaster they would prefer to go down with the ship rather than eke out a few hours or even days or weeks of life in a raft or a life jacket in the ocean. The single-hander who has this view might consider that when the actual moment of decision comes his philosophy may be modified by the reality of events. It is hard for a man to know how he will react when he is faced with a decision which carries the ultimate choice of life itself but in most cases, when it comes to the point, he will choose any course which enables him to go on living, however unpleasantly.

Human nature and the life force invariably combine so that a man will strive to live at all costs – the sea has many tales to offer of incredible feats of survival. Single-handers are likely to be among those who do not give up life lightly and whatever his thoughts may be before he starts, the man alone is wise if he gives himself the option to survive by all the means available.

## Pirates and robbers

The danger of being attacked and robbed or even harmed in some parts of the world is now very real. A man by himself has little defence against modern pirates who can be ruthless and sophisticated in their methods. The violent robbery of yachts has now become a real danger in many of the most beautiful and ideal cruising grounds of the world. There are parts of the world where it is not unusual for a yacht at sea to be boarded and robbed by armed men. There are many parts where it is unsafe for even a crewed yacht to be cruising alone and unprotected. The single-hander must leave his boat alone whenever he goes ashore – she may be at risk in places which were considered quite safe a few years ago. Lying at anchor, where this is possible, is almost always preferable to lying alongside a quay – it is quieter, cleaner, cheaper and safer.

That a yacht should be vulnerable is understandable where there is a huge differential between the rich, or comparatively rich and the poor. In such places a yacht left alone or a yacht with no more than one man on board is a temptation which it is wise not to offer. The single-hander should enquire about this problem before he enters the area and profit from the experience of others. He should be circumspect and take care not to be ostentatious or arrogant when visiting places where the people ashore may not have his own ethical standards and at the same time may be poor. To go ashore expensively dressed and hung about with cameras and binoculars in a smart dinghy with an expensive outboard motor is not tactful, any more than it is sensible to leave the cabin doors open when lying alongside a quay so that anyone walking past can see expensive and desirable objects lying about in the cabin.

Whether to carry firearms on board or not, is every single-hander's own choice. Some believe that to be armed is to be safe and others that the threat of violence begets violence. Firearms must be declared and registered in some foreign ports which often involves tiresome bureaucracy. The single-hander's best defence is his own modesty and unpretentiousness. If it can be seen from his demeanour and from the appearance of his boat that he is a simple man, anxious to be accepted as an ordinary wayfarer and a friend, he is likely to be kindly received and his property respected. If he appears as a rich itinerant whose purpose is only to purchase what the country has to offer and give nothing in return, he may be in some danger.

Perhaps the most delightful feature of sailing alone to foreign parts is the reception accorded to a single-hander. Unlike the tourist who is often regarded only as a source of income, the lone sailor becomes a real part of the place and is a respected, even to some extent an honoured guest. He will be welcomed and liked for as long as his attitude is in sympathy with the people who are his hosts.

# 13 TRIALS OF THE MAN ALONE

Solitude and loneliness are two distinct states, not to be confused one with the other. Solitude, to a man at sea, implies calm contentedness, a fusing of the mind with its surroundings, an acceptance of circumstances and environment, a state of tranquillity. Loneliness implies discontent, a feeling of deprivation, a yearning for company, a frustrated dependence on other human beings, tension. The first state, solitude, is what the single-hander must achieve for himself if his venture is to be successful – if he falls into loneliness he will fail. Solitude is a frail plant which can be upset by adversity – the single-hander's resources of calm and self-discipline, his optimism and his faith in his project will be needed in full measure if solitude is to be nurtured and loneliness kept at bay. Solitude can be shot to pieces by the rigours of the ocean. Bad weather, bad luck, misjudgements or misfortunes can make a man regret that he ever set foot aboard alone, or that he was ever fool enough to sail outside the harbour entrance by himself.

Once he allows doubts to take hold he will begin to feel small and lonely, oppressed by misgivings and only craving another person to share them. Any man can live in solitude when the aspect of the sea and the sky is calm and gracious, but when the body and the mind are stretched by day after day and week after week of the ocean's malice, loneliness creeps in to sap the single-hander's courage and to undermine his will. He will find, when the whole apparatus of the ocean's aggression is turned against him, that his own slight resources, mental and physical, are soon depleted. It is then that he must be on his guard against his own tendency to be lonely. Loneliness in the ocean is a terrifying condition which the single-hander must avoid if he is to keep his reason and his contentment. The mind and his imagination and his physical responses can play tricks when he has been alone for many days in extreme conditions. He may reach a state when his judgements are unbalanced – when he does things which he would not do in ordinary circumstances. He must learn, by experience or perhaps by self analysis, to recognize mental unbalance in himself – he may then be in a position to counteract it. Failing actual experience, even if he has knowledge of the effect an extended period alone in bad weather can have on him, he may be able to develop enough introspection to counter this effect.

## Hypnosis of solitude

It can happen and has happened to many single-handers – Moitessier was a notorious one and Slocum another, that a man will decide after many days alone to change his destination and to continue to a new landfall many days further on. Moitessier sailed round the world in the 1968–9 single-handed race. Homeward bound in the Atlantic, he elected to sail on, past South Africa, across the expanse of the Indian Ocean and so up to the Pacific Islands. He covered 37,455 miles and was at sea for ten months. There is a kind of hypnotic fascination with the ocean and with the life of solitude – the feeling that a man is not of this world at all, but is held away from it and all its people by some extension of time and space – that urges him on and forever on towards more and more distant destinations. Sometimes a man in this state, which is a type of maritime euphoria, is only brought to harbour by necessity – shortage of water or stores or some damage to his boat. The single-hander must beware of this in himself, as well as of other eccentricities, or he may cause distress to others as well as exposing himself to feats of endurance for which he had not planned.

The imagination runs riot when a man is alone. Ideas grow

explosively in the sub-conscious, feeding themselves on solitude and swelling until they fill the spaces of the mind, pushing out rational thought and making it difficult to form sensible judgements – an intellectual intoxication. In normal life the imagination is stimulated naturally by ordinary intercourse with people and things that make up the daily round. For the man alone, all this is taken away from him and a void is left which must fill itself. His own undiluted imagination may not be the best medicine – he will need the artificial stimulus of other people's ideas and thoughts through books and, if he is so inclined, music. A wide and varied course of reading and a bold choice of music will help him to keep a sanely balanced outlook. A man alone has an unique opportunity to widen his intellectual grasp by reading. He should select a span – poetry, philosophy, humour, slapstick, fiction and biography or history – to keep his mind brim full, leaving no spaces to be filled by fantasies of his own which might take an alarming hold of him. He can experiment with his musical grasp, bringing with him unfamiliar works as well as those which may be a part of his life, to explore and discover as he never could ashore, with great profit to himself. He must learn how to feel for himself the pulse of his own mental health.

## Importance of trivialities

The man alone should beware of becoming a slave to the very routine he has himself devised for his own well-being, and he should avoid becoming addicted to inconsequential habits. To take a trivial example, which can none the less inflate itself in the mind of a man alone, he may like a glass of orange-juice at 1100 each day or a can of beer with his lunch. When the juice or the beer runs out he may regard this as a major disaster. He searches the ship for some forgotten supply, cursing and swearing and at the limits of frustration when he can find nothing. He believes, with devastating passion, that he has been overwhelmed by an irreparable misfortune. It is surprising how important such a crisis can seem at the time and how ridiculous afterwards. Another person would dilute his emotional responses and bring them into line with common sense. In place of an orange-juice, lemon or water would serve as well.

It is one of the effects of solitude that the imagination becomes over-wound, racing from imagined misfortune to ruin in a confusion of aimless pessimism while simple truth is forgotten. This disease increases dramatically when conditions are bad and the single-hander is tired. If he can recognize it in himself, he can probably cure it by stimulating his mind with someone else's imagination through the medium of books or music. A book or another person can take him out of the narrow mental tunnel in which he finds himself. There may be other pastimes than music or reading – chess, crossword puzzles, drawing and painting, even writing or performing music which may serve the single-hander as well.

## Frustration

Frustration is an even greater psychological enemy – it can wear a man down and reduce him to a shivering jelly of guilt and delirium. Again, it attacks most fiercely when conditions are bad, and again it can be kept under control if it is recognized and understood. Sometimes everything conspires to irritate – one small annoyance builds on another until suddenly, some further tiny provocation will break the slender barrier between sanity and unbalance and a man will swear and curse with fury, working himself into a genuine rage for the sake of some in-consequential mishap. Women, perhaps because they have less of the ingredient aggression in their psychological make-up, are usually calmer when harassed by frustration. There are a thousand worries to tear out the frayed edges of the solitary sailor's patience.

Changing jibs perhaps, he finds that he has left the shackle key below. He goes to get it leaving the sail in a mound on the foredeck. A rogue breeze gets under it and blows it overboard so that when he reconnects his harness and comes back to the foredeck it is streaming in the water. As he hauls it aboard the bare end of the halyard slips from the cleat and flies aloft, just out of his reach. He stands on the boom, straining up as it swings and blows with the breeze and the yacht's roll. He catches it, triumphantly, but his foot slips and he crashes to the deck, bruising his shin. Without a jib the yacht luffs so that the mainsail shakes and thunders. He runs aft to adjust the vane but is brought up with a jerk, his harness the wrong side of a shroud, like a dog on a lead and a lamp-post. He settles the yacht on course and goes back to the foredeck biting his lip, a mounting tide of fury welling up inside him. He puts up a new sail and now the yacht bears away, threatening a jibe. He runs aft to the helm and trips, falling headlong into the cockpit and catching his head a smart blow. Now his control is gone and he lets fly, cursing his boat with all the language at his command and smiting the tiller with his fist.

Now the single-hander has reached an all-time low in his affairs. As in a knock-out, also after a bout of intense fury, the blood drains from the brain and in a few moments returns with a flush – he regains a state of calm, suffering from remorse, shame, self pity and loneliness. If another person had been on board, his frustration would have been lessened and his behaviour inhibited.

## Use of imagination

It is not easy for a man alone to overcome frustration but it is one of his most urgent tasks. Surprisingly often in a small boat in the ocean and in many different ways, there is a build-up of small, insignificant circumstances which accumulate into a threatening situation. Most important for the single-hander to understand is that it does not in the least matter if he vents his wrath by hurling abuse at the fresh air or even at his boat – both are forgiving media. If it is a way of releasing pent up emotion it is justified and he need feel no guilt or shame – an apology to the boat will set the matter right.

He may find it a help to use his imagination constructively. He can invite an imaginary person to share his life on board, in whom he invests a name, an identity and a personality and this unfortunate can be made into a scapegoat, a chopping-block for his aggression. This person can be abused for his misdeeds with impunity and he can be held responsible for any misfortune or misadventure, preferably in a loud voice, which will echo round the empty spaces of the ocean but which will have a calming and soothing effect on the single-hander. A gremlin aboard as crew will be worth his keep. As a further therapy he should explain the incident to his tape-recorder, together with an account of his behaviour, freely and frankly reporting every detail of what happened. When he plays this to himself the next day it will have a wholesome effect on his ability to control himself.

## Lack of sleep

When things begin to get unpleasant at sea, the first casualty for the single-hander is his sleep. Apprehension and anxiety start a train of mental unease which hits at sleep first and over-tiredness, in turn, increases nervousness and tension in a destructive spiral. Fatigue has many facets. In its early stages it slows the working of the mind and the body, making simple things difficult to grasp and difficult to carry out. Once he is throughly into the routine of a long voyage the man alone should, to some extent be proof against fatigue. He will be used to sleeping at odd hours throughout the day and night, in short snatches and he will have trained his brain to spring up, alert and ready, as soon as he wakes. However, if two or three of his sleep sessions are interrupted he may soon fall into a state of fatigue. Prolonged bad weather, producing discomfort, may be responsible for a serious lack of sleep.

## Discomfort

A boat which leaks through the deck can submit the man alone to a slow and ruinous torture in place of sleep and once the pattern of sleep is interrupted it may be difficult to regain. When spray is continually lashing across the deck, perhaps sailing hard to windward or on a reach in a rough sea, it is a good boat that does not let any in. Time spent in harbour sealing round the coach-roof, skylights and hatches may save days of discomfort. In bad weather when it is cold, water which forces its way into the cabin or is brought in by the single-hander himself through the companion-way, will not evaporate or dry up or simply go away. If bad weather persists over a period of days or weeks slowly everything inside the boat gets wet. In time all bedding is wet, clothes are wet, mattresses are soaked and the cabin takes on a soggy humidity which permeates every pore of the single-hander's body and mind. If it is also cold his distress is many times magnified. Sleeping in these conditions becomes impossible until a state of absolute exhaustion is reached. Instead, the single-hander will fall into a state of lethargy when everything seems impossible and when he may even not be fully aware of his surroundings. He will then be a prey to pessimism, despair and loneliness. He will no longer be properly in command, but will be the prisoner of his environment.

## Dreams and imaginings

Small sailing boats are probably as safe in a storm in the ocean as any vessel. Even if commanded by a man who has been reduced to incompetence by the unending stress of acute discomfort, his boat will probably survive, but extreme fatigue has unnerving emotional effects on the single-hander. He will lose his appetite and will lose his will to look after himself – he will be too lethargic to cook a good meal, it will become difficult for him to keep himself warm, all the jobs he does on deck will be performed slowly and without proper thought. He will be subject to bouts of despair. At the sound of some nostalgic tune on the radio or a sentence in a book which touches some chord in his mind, he will burst into tears and sob uncontrollably. At the extremes of fatigue he may fall into a semi-coma, half awake and half asleep, when hidden and unspoken alarms and fears grope in the half light of his consciousness.

He may dream or imagine that a great ship is speeding towards his yacht, her bulk curving upwards in a tower of steel, the rivets in even rows like disciplined armies, her bow-wave a plume of crystal water swept upwards as she slices the ocean, bearing down on him with limitless, unseeing force. He will wake with a cry, sweating and trembling and will run blindly into the cockpit, waking only in time before he hurls himself into the sea.

Fatigue too, can be foreseen and its effects countered by the single-hander. It is inevitable that he will suffer from stress and anxiety in bad weather or other difficult conditions. He has the responsibility for his ship and his own life firmly on his own shoulders and every action he takes is based on his unaided judgement. This must give him some justifiable cause for anxiety. In bad weather he must learn to observe himself, as it were from a distance, and to gauge the degree of fatigue which he is suffering. If he feels himself slipping into lassitude he must recognize this danger and create the conditions for himself in which he can rest before it is too late and he loses the will to do so.

## Rest and food

If the cabin is becoming wet and uncomfortable he must heave-to, or lie a-try or run before it with warps streamed so that the boat is comfortable and dry enough for him to sleep. If the coach-roof leaks so that inside the boat is a shower bath, he might rig a canvas cockpit cover over it which will keep most of the water out. If he can bring himself to take action before his tiredness becomes a danger to him, it may not happen. Even in a survival storm, if he acts in time the single-hander should be able to maintain himself in good fettle. Hot food and drink, prepared in advance and kept in a flask, is often crucial.

## Trial by calm

Prolonged calm may have as devastating a result on the mental state of a man alone as storm conditions – it will not lead to fatigue but a calm can unhinge mental equilibrium just as surely. In some respects it is more difficult to bear with. The storm demands constant action, some planning and acute awareness and concentration – the calm is outside the scope of any action by the single-hander. He must sit, possessing his soul for day after day, sometimes week after week. He sees his nicely calculated ETA thrown awry, his confidence in a quick passage knocked asunder, his mean average speed brought tumbling down. Worse, he sees his stores ebbing away with no progress to show for it, his water requiring to be measured, even rationed. When the sails are set the gear crashes from side to side as the yacht rolls, the mainsail chafing and wrenching at the bolt ropes all to no purpose. When the sails are down the sun beats on the deck without pity. Nothing he can do or think or say or threaten makes any difference.

In these conditions the single-hander, again, must watch himself carefully. The boredom of it has a cruel twist because he does not know how long or short his ordeal by calm may be. Often there is the aspect of wind – he may even fancy that he sees wind on the horizon, or sometimes quite close to the boat – but it eludes him. He may be tempted to launch a dinghy and row off to observe from a distance the forlorn, silent figure of his boat, rolling and dipping in the swell like some abandoned, archaic relic. The dinghy seems unnatural and unreal perched on this outer skin of ocean like an insect. The sea seems thick and impenetrable so that however he rows he makes no progress through it. He and the dinghy are out of proportion, too insignificant to be considered within this vastness. It is a strange, unnerving experience and the single-hander will hurry back on board to his security.

To swim in a calm ocean is another impulsive desire, acceptable if it is not played with foolishly. He may venture further and always further from the boat, feeling himself vulnerable, unprotected, naked, at risk from any creature yet fascinated by this experiment with the extremes of his own nervous response. He gazes down into the dark, mysterious bowl where light itself is swallowed and reduced by the deepening and thickening blue, its refracted shafts stabbing aimlessly downwards. Then again he feels insecurity grip and he scrambles for the boat, swearing not to do it again.

## Using the engine

Sometimes in the days of sail, crews were put to towing with the boats in prolonged periods of calm, not so much for the progress the ship could make in this way as for the relief of tedium and inactivity. Although its range is small and the distance made of little consequence, the single-hander should use his engine as soon as a calm becomes onerous. Unless he is equipped with electric self-steering he will have to sit and steer his boat for as long as there is no wind to operate the steering vane and this provides useful activity. If he can keep the boat moving, even a short distance every day, the psychological stress of a calm will be much relieved and he may come to a breeze more quickly. If the engine is used in short bursts rather than for long periods, his fuel will last over a greater number of days and the engine will provide the variety and sense of purpose in his life which is essential to him.

Again, a period of calm spent with another person where there is exchange of hopes and fears, can pass without mental strain. It is not easy for the single-hander to come to terms with it, especially when he is new to the business of sailing alone. It takes time for the mind to be attuned to a new concept of living which puts time in a different perspective.

## The time scale

To come to terms with both the calm and the storm is to reach an accommodation with life in the ocean. The single-hander will become aware that in essence, time is not to be measured by the trivial demands of the life he has left behind him but by the great master clock of nature. In reality it is of no consequence to himself or to the world at large whether he crosses the ocean in thirty or in three hundred days – his very survival is irrelevant to the ocean. It is society, not the sea, which sets limits of days and hours. The man alone has cast himself free of these restraints and has taught himself to live without them. His new acquisition, more valid and valuable than any time schedule imposed by society, is the knowledge that he must live out his purpose within the confines of the ocean and her mysteries. He will find in his own mind the resources of truth and calm which can bring him safely and securely to the other side. In a world which is circumscribed by measurements of time the single-hander finds for himself a new and more profound chronometer which will serve him until he reaches the conclusion of his voyage, even of his existence.

## And a question

As to why a man should have the wish and the will to sail alone, the answer is as great an enigma at the end as at the beginning of an enquiry or exposition of how it can most easily and safely be done. There may be as many answers as there are lone sailors. The man who enters a single-handed race is a competitor – perhaps in a different category because although alone, he operates in a group all having the same aim and following the same course. There are publicists who sail for fame, others sail alone for profit and some for stunts. Some are desperate men hoping to snatch success from a last throw, sometimes failing and paying with their lives. Some hope to find a better life where they are masters of their own fates, others have suffered misfortune or deep unhappiness and hope to find solace in the ocean. There are those who seek escape or fulfilment or an inner calm which they believe can be reached through solitude and others again who do not ask themselves and have never asked why, but have sailed alone only because they want to reach their destinations.

To all of them the ocean is mentor and master, disposing to all as equals, taking and giving according to its own immutable laws, the rich, the poor, the humble, the arrogant all heard in the same court and subject to the same judgement. The man or woman who commits himself alone to the sea's mercy will pass through many shades of experience, through the whole span and scope of the ocean's favour. He will come back a wiser man, a stronger man and a more complete man.

# Index

Alarm clock, 21
Anchor, 25, 103, 105–9, 110, 113–14
Anxiety, 22
Awareness, 22

Bandage, 82
Barometer, 45, 54, 58–9, 133
Bermudian rig, 119–20, 125, 130, 133, 137–8, 140, 143–4

Cable stopper, 111–13
Calm, 14–18, 27, 40, 42, 171, 178–81
Chart, 47, 152
Chronometer, 58–9, 62–3, 181
Chum weight. *See* Anchor
Climbing aloft, 146–7
Coasting, 44–5, 48, 54
Collision, 53
Collision regulations, 31
Compass, 58, 60
Concussion, 80, 83–4

D.F. *See* Radio
Dead reckoning, 45–7, 62, 68, 92
Deviation, 60
Diet, 78
Dressing, wound, 83

Echo sounder, 58
Engine, 15, 104, 151, 180
Exercise, 77, 80

Fear, 25
First Aid, 81
Fishing, 159
Fishing boats, 48

Fitness, 77
Firearms, 167, 169–70
Flares, 165, 167
Food, 151–9
Fracture, 84–5
Frustration, 16, 171, 173–5

Gaff, 98, 130, 133, 137–9, 140–3, 145–6
Gale, 12–13, 54, 56, 91, 93–5, 97, 99–100
Grapnel, 116

Hand lead, 73–4
Harness. *See* Safety harness
Hasler, 43
Health, 76–7
Helm. *See* Tiller
Hypnosis, 172

Immunization, 79
Infection, 79
Injury, 80
Inspection, deck, 22

Journal, 57

Ladder, 88
Lamps, 53, 92
Leaks, 161–3, 176
Lifelines, 34–5
Life raft, 165–7
Lights, 49–50, 53
Lloyds, 168
Log book, 44, 46
Log, patent. *See* Patent
Loneliness, 171–2, 175, 177

Mainsail, 124, 131, 139, 143, 144, 146, 179
Mayday, 168
Mitre cut, 130
Mooring, 102

Notebook, 150-3

Oil lights, navigation, 52
Oil, 95
Operation, 80, 82
OSTAR, 32, 172
Oven, 157-8

Pain killer, 79, 85
Paraffin, 52
Patent log, 46-7, 59, 72
Piracy, 169
Plankton, 160
Pressure cooker, 156
Pressure lantern, 50
Pumps, 163-5

Racing, 31-2, 118
Radio, 58, 63, 71
Raft. *See* Life raft
Reefing, 124, 127-8, 131, 134
Riding, John, 118
Rig, 119, 131-2
Runners, 140, 144-5
Routine, 24
R.Y.A., 32

Safety harness, 29, 32, 33-4, 36-9, 40, 66, 131, 167
Sea anchor, 97, 100
Self steering, 43-4
Sextant, 58-9, 63-5
Sharks, 87
Ship-log, 73

Sights, 62-3, 65-9
Signalling lamp, 50
Sixth sense, 22
Sleep, 19-21, 49, 176-7
Slocum, 43, 69
Solitude, 101, 11, 18, 27, 171-3
Speed, 26
Splints, 82, 84-5
Spray, the, 43
Square rig, 119, 123, 137-8
Storm, 13, 27, 56, 90-1, 96, 178, 180
Stores, 149
Stress, 21, 28
Sun awnings, 86
Survival packs, 165
Sutures, 82

Tape-recorder, 58, 74-5, 176
Tiller, 115
Tools, 150
Toothache, 85
Topping lift, 139, 142, 145
Topsail, 139, 147-8
Trade winds, 13, 14, 119, 120, 123, 136
Trysail, 133, 148
Twin staysails, 42, 76, 120-4, 136, 143-6, 148

Vangs, 139, 141-2
Venus, 69
Verey pistol, 167
Voss, 118

Warps, streaming, 94
Water, 158
Weather forecasts, 54
Windlass, 109
Women, 10, 24

184